DATE DUE

FORM 393 SCHOOL SPECIALTY SUPPLY, SALINA, KANSAS

MAR 3'80			
OCT 22 1986			
2/7-87			
JUN 6 - 1987			
JAN 1 0 1998			

BY THE EDITORS OF CONSUMER GUIDE®

Tracing Your ROOTS

10530

Bell Publishing Company
New York

Contents

Copyright ©1977 by Publications International, Ltd.
All rights reserved.
This book may not be reproduced or quoted in whole or in part by mimeograph or any other printed means or for presentation on radio or television without written permission from:
Louis Weber, President
Publications International, Ltd.
3841 West Oakton Street
Skokie, Illinois 60076

Library of Congress Catalog Card Number: 77-92416

This edition published by:
Bell Publishing Company
A Division of Crown Publishers, Inc.
One Park Avenue
New York, N.Y. 10016
By arrangement with Publications International, Ltd.

a   b   c   d   e   f   g   h

Introduction

Family history is fascinating and educational. Designed for the beginner, TRACING YOUR ROOTS provides all the guidelines you need to track down your lineage while avoiding frustrating and discouraging deadends.

For many years family histories were more or less limited to those from aristocratic or wealthy backgrounds. Today, however, things are completely different. Reconstructing the family tree has become the favorite leisure activity of hundreds of thousands of enthusiastic people. Every family has a fascinating story to tell.

The United States is populated by the descendants of courageous pioneers — men and women who left their homelands and set off on the adventure of a new land. They came from around the world, walking across the Bering Strait in prehistoric times and daring the Atlantic in fragile sailing ships. They came from all walks of life — nobles and peasants, craftsmen and farmers, refugees and scoundrels. Who they were and who their descendants are is a genealogical mystery, but one that can be solved by digging into the past.

Names and places that once seemed remote come vividly to life when you discover their connection with your own family. Perhaps your great-grandmother waved a flag at Queen Victoria's Diamond Jubilee.

Did your ancestors help storm the Bastille? Sail on a China Clipper? Fight at the Little Big Horn? Escape from the Cossacks?

TRACING YOUR ROOTS is designed as a guide to this exciting hobby, one that will help you discover your progenitors. It contains all the basic information you will need to get started. You will learn by doing, proceeding step by step from the known to the unknown.

Since you are the person you know the most about, you begin with yourself. Once you have collected some documents and mementos, you need a system to keep them organized and readily accessible. An efficient filing system lets you know at a glance what information you have found and what blank spots you have to fill. The ancestry chart and the individual and family information sheets are the heart of your collection. They are a summary of your research, containing the most important data you have discovered.

You can gather a surprising amount of information from family resources. Photograph albums, diaries, and old letters give you the "feel" of the period, revealing the attitudes and thoughts of the men and women of the past. Elderly relatives are usually delighted to recount anecdotes about their youth.

Before you take the next step — hunting through the records themselves — it's a good idea to become familiar with some of the legal and technical terms you will encounter in old documents. This will make the records much easier to understand and save you a lot of time later on.

The first place to look is in the federal census records. They will provide all sorts of useful facts that give you leads to your next stop. Local, state, and federal archives contain enormous amounts of information. Once you know what records are available and how to get at them, you will make good progress.

Frustrating deadends can often be avoided if you are alert to potential problems. In the course of time, boundaries are altered, names are modified or spelled differently, and people move from one locale to another, perhaps changing occupations or religions along the way. Even dates can be puzzling because of shifts from one calendar system to another.

At the end of each chapter, you'll find important reference sources, suggestions for further reading, and where to write for the documents and records discussed.

Just for fun, we've included a chapter on heraldry. You'll learn the basic terms and traditions of this art, and find ideas for creating your own coat of arms.

You're Number One

The basic principle of genealogical research is to work from the known to the unknown. The place to start is with yourself — the person you know the most about. Here are the best ways of organizing the documents you collect and the most efficient methods of keeping track of your information.

Poland 1920

Start tracing your roots by gathering any family information you may have near at hand. Collect names. While your primary interest at the beginning will be to identify your direct or lineal ancestors, the individuals who have been responsible for producing you, the rest of the family is interesting too. The families of your direct ancestors, such as their brothers and sisters, your collateral ancestors, should also be collected. The more names you have the better, since many times you will be able to find additional information about a direct ancestor from the records of their aunts, uncles, brothers, and sisters. Collect names and keep adding to them. Keep them alphabetized and right at hand. You can never tell when checking on one of the cousins will bring in the rest of the family.

Collect family pictures and other memorabilia. Begin labeling right away, being careful not to damage articles. If you can not identify the people in the pictures, ask around. If everyone agrees, put the information on the back. If everyone disagrees, put the information on the back anyway; but identify who said

Chicago, Illinois 1930

Chicago, Illinois 1917

Chicago, Illinois 1880

9

Louisiana
1900

Chicago, Illinois 1880

you. What the system is, is not as important as having one.

The first consideration is keeping everything together in one place. The second is keeping things where you can find them when you need them. Start with a sturdy box or carton which will hold all the materials you collect and your supplies. A cardboard box, the kind that is used for storing files, works very well. It is too large to get lost and yet small enough to carry. After you have the box, get an envelope or file folder for each family name and write the name on the outside of the envelope or on the tab. As you get more information you will need more envelopes — perhaps one for each individual member of the family. An 8½ x 11-inch three-ring binder filled with lined and unlined paper is useful for keeping track of what you have done and where you have been and it can also serve as a log. It is just as important to record what you don't find as to record what you do. If you don't find a reference to a certain member of your family you thought might be mentioned in a book, jot it down — it will save you from making the same search again. Sometimes you will find piles of material in a few hours, while at other times weeks may pass with only negative results. On the lined paper keep a list of the records you have searched, the books you have checked, and the information you have found. You can also keep an index to all the names you have collected, arranged alphabetically by last name. Include dates for ease in identification. The unlined paper is useful for making sketches or drawing maps.

After you have worked on your family for a while, you may find that some "facts" are better than others. Always be just a bit skeptical about even the most impressive "fact." Just because something is printed does not mean that it is so, nor are records written in Bibles, prayerbooks, or beautifully bound "Our Family" books always the last word. When copying these records check for the date the book was published. It is nice to know that so-and-so was born September 15, 1779, but if the book was not printed until 1864 the information could not have been entered at the time of the event. Similarly, if all the names and dates for a hundred years are written in the same handwriting and in the same color ink, you might suspect that they were either copied from another source or being done from memory. Entries that appear to have been recorded at the time of the event are usually more reliable.

The reliability of an item of information depends on who gave it in the first place. The information on a marriage license is usually given by the individuals themselves at a time when their memory should be clear. On the other hand, information on a death certificate is given by a relative or a neighbor.

Sometimes different records show different dates for the same event. If a birth certificate and census record agree on the date, the evidence supporting that date would be strong. If, on the other hand, the census record says Mary is 40 and her birth certificate suggests she should be 53, look for additional

what. People can remember the same occasion differently. A mother will tell you how beautiful her daughter looked and a father will remember how much the wedding cost. Start gathering material before it is forgotten or lost.

In a short time you will have accumulated a number of photographs and a number of pieces of paper. You will need some kind of system to keep them straight. For most people the importance of a system is impressed upon them after they have lost or misplaced a document. Work out a system that is comfortable to

Chicago, Illinois 1905

Niles, Michigan 1885

sources. Just because a birth certificate comes from the county clerk's office doesn't make it 100 percent correct, but a photocopy of the original document is probably more accurate than a typed copy.

While part of the fun and excitement of working on family history is finding nuggets of buried treasure, don't jump to conclusions.

Today there are many courses and workshops on family history being offered. The better ones are those given by genealogical and patriotic organizations. At them you can meet other people who are tracing their own family histories. You can share information with them and possibly combine forces if you are both searching in the same area.

There may be times when the particular records you need are not available in your area and the distance is too great for you to search them in person. In this case you might consider hiring somebody to do your searching for you. There are advantages and disadvantages. The obvious advantage is that that individual is on the spot, is familiar with the records, and is willing to do the search. Check with the librarian, county clerk, or a member of a genealogical so-

ciety in that area for their suggestions on possible searchers. The disadvantages are that it can be expensive (always reach a definite understanding ahead of time as to fees and expenses) and that you will miss out on the fun of the search.

Now that you have collected your thoughts and some material and have a place to keep them, you are ready to start filling out the charts.

Suggested Reading

Doane, Gilbert H.: *Searching for Your Ancestors: The How and Why of Genealogy,* ed. 4. Minneapolis, University of Minnesota Press, 1973.

Jacobus, Donald Lines: *Genealogy as Pastime and Profession,* rev. ed. Baltimore, Genealogical Publishing Co., 1971.

Stryker-Rodda, Kenn: *Genealogy.* North Brunswick, New Jersey: Boy Scouts of America, Merit Badge Series, 1973.

Williams, Ethel W.: *Know Your Ancestors: A Guide to Genealogical Research.* Rutland, Vermont, Charles E. Tuttle Co., 1960.

Filling Out the Charts

You are probably familiar with genealogical charts such as those used to illustrate the family trees of English royalty. An ancestry chart works the other way around. It begins with you and traces backward. The individual and family information sheets make all your data available at a glance.

Charts and worksheets are important because they organize your information. They are a working blueprint of your family history — not the family history itself. They give names, places, dates, and relationships. Charts and worksheets become a part of your permanent records. They organize information so that it's easier to record and find.

Here are a few important points to consider in filling out the charts and worksheets: (1) Use a pencil when you start. If changes have to be made it is easier to erase than to scratch out. You can fill in with ink later. (2) Always use an individual's full original name — for both men and women. All name changes are recorded on the individual information sheets. (3) Give day, month, and year for all dates. Use the name of the month rather than a numeral, and don't reduce the year to the last two numbers — this can lead to confusion.

Ancestry Chart

Ancestry charts, lineage charts, pedigree charts, and progenitor charts all refer to the same thing (see the charts at the end of the book). This is the chart on which you record your direct ancestors. Since this is your chart, start right in and write your full name on line 1. Use the name you were born with. Indicate name changes on your individual sheet. Below your name fill in your date and place of birth. Then fill in as many of the other blanks as you can. Don't be disturbed if you cannot fill much out. Most people can't go beyond their own name without doing some checking.

On the ancestry chart, notice that number 2 is the father and number 3 is the mother of number 1. Fathers are always given first and mothers second.

The father's number is always double that of his child and the mother's number is double that of her child plus one. The numbers for men are always even (except for number 1 which can be used by both sexes) and those for women are always odd.

This ancestry chart records five generations and can be extended by adding more charts to accommodate everyone you find. When you add a new chart (beginning where chart one ends) all individuals retain their original numbers. Individual 16 on chart one becomes individual 16 on chart two. His father becomes 32 and his mother becomes 33. Individual 17 on chart one becomes individual 17 on chart three and her parents would be 34 and 35.

There are many forms of ancestry charts. Some are arranged into trees or fans, which are quite decorative, but the one in this book is easy to read and can be extended indefinitely without any trouble.

After you have gone as far as you can with the ancestry chart, turn to the individual information sheets.

Individual Information Sheets

On an individual information sheet you record information on one of the individuals listed on your ancestry chart. Take the appropriate name and number from the ancestry chart and put them at the top of the individual information sheet. Under "Nicknames or Name Changes" list names by which the individual has been known and give the approximate dates if possible.

Give the original names of the parents and the individual information sheet numbers where more information about them can be found. List all marriages of this individual in the order in which they took place, even if there were no children. Indicate whether the marriage was ended by death, divorce, desertion, or any other cause. Give the first names of children and mark with a star any child that appears on the ancestry chart. Add information to the chart whenever you discover more. On the reverse side of the individual information sheet, show the sources where you obtained the information for the statements on the front. There may be more than one source and all sources may not agree. Make sure you include enough identification so you will be able to use this sheet as a reference when you are out searching. The copies of the documents themselves should be filed in the individual's folder which you leave at home.

For example, if there is a divorce, give court and docket number. Under jobs and occupations, list professional certification and union memberships. Under residences, give tax receipts or voters' list and, finally, under records, give references to documents — such as a will, guardianship records (if minor child or incompetent), and the distribution of the estate — and where they can be found.

After the information has been recorded on the individual information sheet, you will record much of the same information on the family information sheets.

The same information is arranged on the different sheets for different reasons.

Family Information Sheets

The family information sheet shows three generations: one man and one woman, their parents, and their children. On the reverse side record documentation on each of the children. Mark the individual that appears in the ancestry chart with a star. Charts and information sheets are designed to help. From time to time evaluate the information you are putting down. If you have a man becoming a father at 83 or getting married at 9, take another look. You may have the wrong person, there may have been an error in copying, or you may have an unusual situation. Put down information as you find it even if "facts" don't agree. Don't try to make the "facts" fit.

If the search for ancestral roots is to be meaningful, it should be more than a collection of names, dates, and places. People must be fleshed out with as much detail as you are able to discover so that their personalities can be revealed. You may discover that your talent for art, music, mechanics, or other professions has come from one or more ancestors.

Wisconsin 1875

Los Angeles, California 1895

13

Beach, North Dakota 1912

Poland 1915

Family Resources

You possess more documentation than you think — photograph albums, letters and diaries, wedding and birth certificates. All of these can provide valuable clues about names, dates, and places in your family saga. An elderly relative may prove to be a treasure trove of family traditions.

Family history is family business. Let everyone in the family know you are working on it. After you have jotted down all you can remember and dug out the old photos that remind you of aunts, uncles, and cousins you haven't thought of in years, drop them a note or give them a call. Ask if they know whether anyone is working on the story of the family and whether a family history has been written or a genealogy published. Kaminkow's bibliography of family genealogies (see list at the end of "Where Do We Go From Here?") in the Library of Congress doesn't include everything. Someone may have a family history that has been privately printed or perhaps a hand-written record done by Great-Aunt Agnes who was inspired by the Centennial. If you find any kind of written family history you have something to start with. Read its introduction, check the indexes (there may be more than one), and then go through the whole book. Family histories vary in accuracy, but in any case it is easier to have something to check than to start completely from scratch.

While you are talking with people ask if they have any old letters, diaries, trophies, photos, or other family mementos. Bibles, missals, and prayerbooks are often mines of information. Don't look only in the front where formal family information was often recorded but also between the pages. Obituaries, letters, marriage contracts, memorial cards, and other precious stuff can often be found. When asking don't forget about baby books, financial records, health and hospital records, wills, deeds, newspaper clippings, class yearbooks, and report cards. Ask them to take a look

Lake View, Illinois 1888

in their safe deposit boxes too. People often forget about these records unless especially reminded.

Another way to collect information is to send out a form letter to all your known relatives. This will give you names of relatives you may not have known you had and may identify other members of the family that are also collecting information.

Write a covering letter and then, on a separate page, ask the questions you would like to have answered with room for people to fill in the information. This makes it much easier for them. Whatever makes it easier will increase the chance of getting an answer. Include a long envelope with a stamp and your address already on it. This self-addressed, stamped envelope is often abbreviated SASE in ads.

Keep copies of all the letters you write. Many people don't mind answering once, but become irate if they get the same letter twice. Some of these members of the family could become future friends, so get off to a good start.

Don't ask for everything they have. They may have boxes of material and if you have offered to pay for copies or shipping you may be facing a large bill. If people offer you material to copy, photocopy it and return the originals right away.

Set up interviews. Before starting, ask permission to take notes and tape the stories. Taping makes it possible to let others hear the stories too. If you are friendly and explain you just want to be sure to get it right, there is usually no objection. When talking with relatives, don't ask them to tell you everything they know about everyone right at the start. That only wears them out. Run your interview like a talk show. Let them talk while you listen. Ask one question at a time, preferably questions that can not be answered by a simple yes or no. Don't challenge or contradict — you can always check the information out later. If you are puzzled, ask for clarification. If what is said to you is unclear, repeat it back and ask if that was what they meant. Don't worry when people wander a bit from the subject. It is hard to stop them without hurting their feelings and they often may end up talking about an interesting, important subject you wouldn't have known enough to ask about.

Some good questions to start with are: "What is your earliest memory?" "What do you remember about your parents and grandparents?" "Where did you live when you were little?" Don't ask delicate, sensitive questions until you know each other well and perhaps not even then unless they volunteer. Instead, ask about family fun, customs at holidays, job and work experience, vacations, what they did for fun, religious activities, hard times, best friends, interesting neighbors, military service, and courting habits. Ask what they feel has changed for the better and for the worse and what their suggestions would be to younger people for a good life.

Be sure you keep your promises and your appointments and if they loan you any material for copying be sure to return it right away.

Whenever possible, have them identify people and places in photographs. If they can, have them take you to the spot where the old family place used to be or walk you through a cemetery. Although family stories, like wine and cheese, improve with age, it is so much easier when someone knows and can tell you rather than your having to reconstruct information and locations from the records. When someone gives you information in confidence, respect it. You have the responsibility of being discreet.

An excellent booklet on how to interview and record family history is *An Oral History Primer* by Gary L. Shumway and William G. Hartley.

Stop while you are both enjoying the experience. Chat a bit before leaving. You may even set up an appointment for a second time around. This will give people a chance to remember more stories — and give them the pleasure of an additional visit. When you do go, leave a self-addressed postcard in case they think of something important just after you leave.

Suggested Reading

Shumway, Gary L., and Hartley, William G.: *An Oral History Primer*. Salt Lake City, privately printed, 1973.

Learning the Language

In the course of your genealogical search, you are likely to come across a wide variety of legal documents — wills, naturalization papers, land grants, and the like. There are important terms you will need to know — words whose meanings will be your key into the past.

Chicago, Illinois 1902

Chicago, Illinois 1877

Chicago, Illinois 1894

As you enter the world of archives, libraries, courts, and courthouses, you may find that an unfamiliar language is used; knowing the precise meaning of these words can help a lot in determining what's going on. As you go back in time, you may find some words that have changed in meaning. In the colonial period, for example, "lumber" meant junk, disused articles, and useless odds and ends that took up room. The term was transferred to the wood and timber that cluttered up the area and, in time, planks that were prepared for sale. A gossip was once a person who acquired spiritual affinity with another by acting as a baptismal sponsor. Mothers and godmothers were gossips, as were fathers and godfathers. Gradually the word came to mean light talk, social conversation of the kind indulged in by friends. Still later, it developed a negative sense of unrestrained tattling and the person who indulged in it. If you are in doubt as to the exact meaning of a word, use a dictionary that was published about the same time as the document in which the word was used. Using a dictionary of the period is important not only in English, but in foreign languages as well.

Glossary

Administrator (female, administratrix): The person appointed by a court to settle the estate of a deceased person.

Alien: An individual who is not a citizen of the country in which he lives.

Attest: To affirm that something is true, correct, or genuine.

Banns: The spoken or published notice of an intended marriage.

Bounty: Money paid by a city or town to volunteers for army service as an inducement to serve.

Bounty land: Land given by the government as a bounty.

Beach, North Dakota 1911

Bounty land warrant: A right to a specific number of acres of unallocated public land granted for military service.

Codicil: A supplement to a will.

Collateral ancestor: A relative not in the direct line, such as the brother, sister, niece, nephew, aunt, or uncle of a direct ancestor.

Competent: Legally qualified or able to act.

Consanguineous: Of the same blood; descended from a common ancestor.

DAR: Abbreviation for the National Society, Daughters of the American Revolution.

Declaration of intention: The first paper or sworn statement made by an alien who intends to become a citizen.

Dower: The legal right of a wife to use or own a portion of her husband's estate (the percentage varies from place to place and from time to time) should she survive him.

Executor (female, executrix): A person designated in a will and appointed by a court to carry out the provisions of the will.

Fee simple: Land in which the inheritor has unqualified ownership.

Fee tail: Land in which the inheritance is limited to particular heirs.

Grantor: A person who gives or sells real property. The person who makes or gives a grant.

Holographic will: A handwritten will.

Indenture: Any deed, sealed agreement, or written contract. A contract by which one person was bound to serve another.

Indentured servant: A person who bound himself for a number of years to pay a debt. A frequent form of indenture was made between emigrants and the captain of the ship on which they sailed. The indentures were then sold at ports of entry.

Infant: Any person not of legal age.

Intestate: Having died without leaving a will; a person who died without leaving a will.

Inventory: A list of all the goods and valuables in an estate which executors and administrators are required to make and file.

Lineal ancestor: A direct ancestor.

Loyalist (sometimes known as United Empire Loyalist): A colonist who remained loyal to Great Britain during the Revolutionary War.

Nuncupative will: An oral will made before witnesses (often a deathbed will) and later written down by someone other than the testator.

Patent: A conveyance of land title by a government.

Patentee: A person who received a land title from a government.

Posthumous: Occurring after an individual's death.

Redemptioner: A person who paid for his passage by becoming an indentured servant.

Relict: Usually a widow.

Restricted records: Records whose use may sometimes be limited.

Testator: A person leaving a will in force at the time of his death.

Making Sense Out of the Census

Every ten years the federal government conducts a census to determine the number of inhabitants and general information about the population. Some of these records go back to 1790 and they are the best place to begin your research and find new leads.

After you have checked out your family resources, the next step is to go to the federal census records. The censuses since 1850 give names, dates, ages, and relationships for all the people living at the same location. The U.S. census records have the advantage of being readily available and probably give more genealogical information than any other documents. In addition, census information is acceptable evidence for Social Security and other instances where age, place of birth, and family relationships must be proven.

Censuses are not new. The word census comes from the Latin *census,* meaning registration of citizens, which in turn comes from *censere,* meaning to assess or tax. A census is a count of people, animals, and property. Censuses are made by countries, cities, states, schools, or other official groups.

The Old Testament tells us that the Lord spoke to Moses in the wilderness and had him do a census. This census included counts by tribe and even information on men 20 years old and up who were able to go to war (Numbers 1:2).

Jesus' birth in Bethlehem was due to the decree of Caesar Augustus that everyone should go back to his own city to be registered for taxation (Luke 2:3).

William the Conqueror ordered a census (the *Domesday Book*) in 1085. From 1600 to 1789, censuses were made in the colonies from time to time under the supervision of the colonial governors.

The first federal enumeration in the United States, the 1790 census, and the following censuses made every ten years, were ordained in Article One, Section 2, of the U.S. Constitution to determine how many representatives (based on population) each state was entitled to have in the House of Representatives.

Double-Checking

When you start working with census records, remember the information is only as good as the people who gave it. Who answered the door and gave the enumerators the information? Perhaps one of the children, or perhaps there was suspicion about the federal employee asking all those fool questions. You will also find cases of women who only aged six years from one census to the next.

It is a good idea to check three consecutive censuses — 1850, 1860, and 1870 or 1860, 1870, and 1880 — to see if the information given is consistent. As a double-check, you can also look at the information given by the brothers of the individual you are primarily interested in. A year's difference one way or the other can often be explained by the date on which the census was taken. Was it taken before or after an individual's birthday?

Whenever you are copying information from a microfilm, notice whether the material is as originally recorded. When the material has been copied or transcribed, there is always an additional chance for error. When you copy information, copy it exactly as it appears in the record. If in doubt about a letter or a figure, put what you think it might be in square brackets: 5 [3]; B [u] ll. To get the information on the heading of the schedule, you may have to go back several pages. The heading will give the count, the township, the page, and the enumerator. Sometimes the same page number may be used on several sheets. When you have found the individual or family you are looking for, record the line number since it will make it easier to go back to the same source.

Soundex

One of the great things done by the Works Project Administration in the 1930's was producing indexes to some of the U.S. census records. The system called Soundex is a boon to searchers since it brings together surnames which sound the same or similar, but which may be spelled differently. The surnames are

Blachleysville, Ohio 1917

Elmhurst, Illinois 1932

all arranged by the Soundex code and then by first names which are arranged alphabetically. To find the Soundex code for the name in which you are interested, write down the name. Next, write down the initial letter and strike out all the vowels and the letters Y, W, and H. The letters that are left are given numerical designations:

1 = B, F, P, V
2 = C, G, J, K, Q, S, X, Z
3 = D, T
4 = L
5 = M, N
6 = R

Double letters and any two letters with the same numerical designation that come together are treated as one letter. Only three numbers are used after the initial letter. Other letters are ignored. If there are less than three letters after the initial letter, zeroes are used to fill out the spaces.

Prefixes (such as van, von, de, di, dela, and du) are sometimes disregarded in alphabetizing and coding, so you may have to check under both Soundex codings. The index is arranged by state and under the state the rolls are arranged by code. It will save time if you code names before asking to see the Soundex indexes to the 1880 and 1900 censuses. Sometimes the name code will cover more than one reel. In that case, if you are looking for Thomas and the break, for example, is at Harriet, you ask for the second reel. If the name is Amy, you ask for the first one. When you find the index card for the name you are looking for, be sure you take down all the information on county,

THE SOUNDEX SYSTEM

Original Name		Step 1		Step 2		Soundex Code
ALSHABKHOU	=	ALSBK	=	ALSB	=	A421
BONANATA	=	BNNT	=	BNT	=	B530
COE	=	C	=	C	=	C000
SCHROEDER	=	SCRDR	=	SCRD	=	S263
YAMAMOTO	=	YMMT	=	YMT	=	Y530
ZIMMERMANN	=	ZMMRMNN	=	ZMRM	=	Z565

township, enumerator, page, and line. Under a single enumerator, there may be more than one page with the same number, so if you don't find the name on the first sheet with the number you are looking for, see if there are others.

An additional and very helpful use of Soundex is collecting spelling variations which you can use when searching other records.

The Individual Censuses

The following paragraphs will tell you what information was collected in the different censuses. Remember, though, the schedule you are interested in may be missing, the individual may not appear, or the information given may be incomplete.

The Census of 1790 — The taking of the first U.S. census was approved March 1, 1790, with the counting to begin on the first Monday in August 1790. The work was to be finished in nine months. Enumerators were hard to find; the pay was very low and no paper or forms were supplied. Part of the census was even recorded on wallpaper. The census records for Maryland and North Carolina are not complete. Those of Delaware, Georgia, and Kentucky, New Jersey, Tennessee, and Virginia were burned during the War of 1812. A partial census for Virginia was later reconstructed from tax rolls. Vermont was not done until 1791, and other states were slow in sending in the information to the federal government. Only men and heads of households are named. Women (except for those who headed households), children, and slaves are merely counted. What is now the District of

1880 CENSUS — UNITED STATES

STATE _____ COUNTY _____ TOWN _____ TOWNSHIP _____ P.O. _____ REFERENCE SOURCE _____

PAGE	DWELLING NO.	FAMILY NO.	NAMES	COLOR	SEX	AGE PRIOR TO JUNE FIRST	MONTH OF BIRTH IF BORN IN CENSUS YR.	RELATIONSHIP TO HEAD OF HOUSE	SINGLE	MARRIED	WIDOWED-DIVORCED	MAR. IN CENSUS YR.	OCCUPATION	MON. UNABLE TO WK.	SICK	BLIND	DEAF AND DUMB	IDIOTIC	INSANE	MAIMED, CRIPPLED	SCHOOL DURING YR.	CANNOT READ	CANNOT WRITE	PLACE OF BIRTH	PLACE OF BIRTH— FATHER	PLACE OF BIRTH— MOTHER

Columbia is included in the Maryland records for Montgomery and Prince Georges counties.

In 1905, when the original was in danger of crumbling away, the 1790 census was printed and indexed in volumes now available in many libraries. A microfilm of this printed census is available. In addition, there is a microfilm of the original records. Since some material in the original 1790 census was left out in the transcribing and some material was transcribed incorrectly, it pays to check the microfilm of the original.

The Censuses From 1800 to 1840 — These records only name heads of households, but changes — such as a husband being replaced by a wife — can suggest other places to check (wills, marriage records, etc.). The 1840 census also lists military pensioners by name and age. Wisconsin is included with Michigan in the 1820 and 1830 censuses.

The Censuses From 1850 to 1870 — The 1850 census is the first to record the names of all persons in the household, and asks for state, country, or territory of birth of all free members of the household. This census contains many errors, probably because so many nosy questions were being asked and many people were suspicious that the census was going to be used for taxing purposes. The 1850 and 1860 censuses have separate slave schedules. The three censuses also include property values, which can lead to wills or local histories, and information on literacy — if your great-great-grandfather couldn't read or write, don't waste time looking for his letters. In the 1860 census, Nevada is listed with Utah, Oklahoma with Arkansas, Wyoming with Nebraska, and Colorado with Kansas.

The Census of 1880 — A partial index, covering only households with children no older than 10 years, is available on Soundex. The records themselves include the relationship of each member of the household to the head of the family and the alleged states or countries of birth of the parents of each listed individual.

The Census of 1890 — More than 99 percent of this census was destroyed by fire in 1921. Fragments remain for parts of Alabama, the District of Columbia, Georgia, Illinois, Minnesota, New Jersey, New York, North Carolina, Ohio, South Dakota, and Texas.

The Censuses of 1900 and After — The census records back to 1900 are restricted. Under certain conditions the Bureau of the Census will answer specific requests about persons listed on them. The Soundex index and the schedules for the 1900 census can be viewed at the regional branches of the National Archives.

Mortality Schedules

For the censuses of 1850, 1860, 1870, and 1880 and for the limited census of 1885, there are mortality schedules which give information on individuals and cause of death in the 12 months preceding the date the census taking was to start (one year out of ten).

The schedules are set up by county — when indexed, they are indexed by states as a whole. In 1918-1919 these schedules were offered back to the states and those that were not claimed were given to the Daughters of the American Revolution and are kept in their library in Washington, DC. Most, but not all, have been indexed and some have been transcribed. These are now available on microfilm at regional branches of the National Archives. Nearly all 1890 census mortality schedules were destroyed by fire in 1921; the 1900 mortality censuses were destroyed before World War I. Since 1900, mortality records have been collected directly from the states.

If the individuals you are interested in died before 1885 during the 12-month period prior to a census, you may find an added bit of information. Creative spelling in entries for cause of death, such as "new money fever" (pneumonia fever) and "no fisian tendin" (no physician attending), will keep you on your toes.

Using the Census Records

Indexes to many of the records have been printed. Where no index is available, search the census records themselves. Remember that every census has some parts missing, that counties are not always arranged alphabetically, and that names may have changed over the years. City records are arranged by ward. Maps of the same period as the census you are using can supply this information.

The federal censuses from 1790 to 1890 that have survived are available on microfilm. These rolls can be purchased from the National Archives at a moderate cost per roll. They can also be borrowed through your local library (make sure your library has a microfilm reader) or the genealogical branch libraries of the Latter-Day Saints. If you are near to a regional branch of the National Archives, you can examine them there (call ahead to make sure that the films you want to see are available and that a microfilm reader will be free). In some centers it is important to make a reservation to avoid a long wait or the disappointment of not being able to view the film in which you are interested.

Requests for print-outs from the censuses done between 1790 and 1890 can be made on Form 7029 from the National Archives.

Reading and Reference Suggestions

Federal Population Censuses, 1790-1890, containing a roll listing and the price for each roll, is available on request (National Archives).

Federal Population and Mortality Census Schedules in the National Archives and the States, special list 24.

U.S. Bureau of the Census: *A Century of Population Growth From the First Census of the United States to the Twelfth, 1790-1900.* GPO, 1909. Reprinted, Baltimore, Genealogical Publishing Co., 1967.

Getting It From the Record

Local, state, and federal archives contain an enormous amount of information — most of it just gathering dust. Finding the specific records you need can be quite a challenge, but it is worth the effort.

Wisconsin 1870

After you have gathered together as much information as you can find, after you have talked to your relatives, read their letters, made notes on all the clues suggested by everything from the heirloom coverlet to the silver spoon, and seen the census where grandpa was listed as a small boy, it is time to check and verify information, even though there still may be many blanks to fill.

The traces of the people you are looking for can be found in many different records. Since people who kept the records were human, too, expect all degrees of accuracy — several records have to be taken together before you can be rather certain about any "fact."

There are marriage records, birth and death records, land records, naturalization records, probate records (wills, estates, and guardianships), court records (civil and criminal), city directories, and county histories. The information is located in many different places. Sometimes records were not required to be kept, sometimes they were destroyed in a fire or a flood, and sometimes records are available but illegible — the ink has faded or the part you want has been torn or eaten away. Photocopies can sometimes be misleading when flyspecks or fuzz in the machine are printed along with the text.

Just because material is in a public place or because it is printed doesn't mean that it is true. Many people feel that if something is printed it must be gospel — not so. Names of people, communities, counties, rivers, parks, and mountains all change. Boundaries change and information on a certain location at different times may be kept in different places.

Fortunately everyone has left some record somewhere. The cycle of birth, marriage, children, and finally death has been repeated generation after generation. One of the reasons to keep accurate records of the birth and marriage of all family members is the

Chicago, Illinois 1933

Chicago, Illinois 1884

23

opportunity it affords to gather information by less direct means.

Birth, marriage, and death — the vital records — are filed initially in the office of the city or town clerk who has jurisdiction over the area where the event occurred. For a specified fee, certified copies can be obtained by mail if sufficient information to identify the particular record being requested is included. For information on where to write for vital statistics records, booklets can be purchased from the Superintendent of Documents.

The registration of American living abroad since 1906 has been the responsibility of U. S. consular posts and should include the person's full name, date and place of birth, identification of spouse, and the name, date, and place of birth of all children. The record volumes are indexed and kept by the State Department. As always, the degree and accuracy of the information depends on who did the transcribing. Spellings can be rather innovative.

Vital records less than 75 years old are not apt to have been published and must be obtained either by mail or in person from the designated city or town clerk or from the appropriate state agency. Everyone wants to know your birth date. It has been recorded with Social Security, on credit and employment applications, and sometimes even in the code of a driver's license. Your residence may be listed on the voters' and tax lists and in the telephone book.

Other records of the county which contain personal information might be land records — the grantor and the grantee indexes, the survey maps and the mortgage records, the probate, guardianship, and related files, and the important orders or miscellaneous records which can include anything from adoption and petitions for financial assistance to small claims or naturalizations granted. They must usually be requested from the clerk in charge.

Many public records offices have converted their earlier records to either microfilm or microfiche. In New York state, a law provides that each county must have a county historian, even though most cities, towns, and villages also have one.

You will be dealing with a new world. Many of the people in it don't give a hoot about the work you are doing and they have other concerns and responsibilities. Keep cool and keep smiling and remember that you are not the only person in the world.

When writing, keep your letters clean, concise, and courteous. Busy people don't have time to go through long rambling letters. The clerks and record custodians are employed to take care of the current, daily business of the office and not to do family histories. Before you go to an office in the city hall or county court house, know exactly what you are going to look for and where you expect to find it. Plat maps are usually kept with deeds, guardianship papers with adoption, and small claims and petitions for assistance in the court records. The year the record was created may also determine where it will be found. When going back in time, use *The Handy Book For*

Albuquerque, New Mexico 1915

Genealogists which includes state and county maps and their histories. Always try to use a map or atlas contemporary with the period. Large counties were often divided up as their population increased.

In 1942 the Works Progress Administration published the Federal Writers Project books on many of our states. These books gave detailed information on local history, geology, geography, culture, agriculture, architecture, education, religion, government, and historic sites, and provide directions on how to reach them.

The WPA also published a survey of the historical records and their locations for most states which is available in most larger libraries.

The libraries and historical societies in the area of your search may be custodians of both published and unpublished data from local records. Volunteers have copied marriage, birth, and death records, deeds and tax lists, and cemetery and probate records. There may be mistakes, but even original records can contain errors.

A city, village, or county is just another area until you have read something of its history. Your ancestors lived there; they had the same frustrations, anxieties, hopes, and joys that you experience. The town's history was part of their life: their children attended school (another record); their money was deposited and withdrawn (and some banks are permitting old records to be copied). The doctor treated

Elmhurst, Illinois 1925

Chicago, Illinois 1890

colds and appendicitis and recorded his patients' names in his day book (which may now be in the library or historical society).

During the later part of the 19th century and the first part of the 20th, local and county histories were written and sold on a subscription basis. In addition to the history of the area, they also contained biographical sketches of "prominent" citizens, usually produced from material supplied by the individual. Contemporary data were basically accurate since everyone else in the area knew the individuals involved, but sometimes the family history or tradition should be salted before swallowing. If your relative decided against buying a book, then his biography would probably not be included. Check other members of the family: a sister's husband might have graciously mentioned something about his wife's family. Local histories may not be completely accurate, but they can often provide colorful details and suggest other places to search. However, don't put today's interpretation on yesterday's events. Try and keep contemporary with the period in which you are working.

Visit and support your local historical society. It usually has local histories and old newspapers. If it has newspaper indexes, double-check in the paper itself. It's fun to find references to birth, marriage, or death in the local paper. If you have time, page through and you may find loads of other information about what was going on between these three main events. Local histories often have pictures of the community and maps. They contain information about important events; they may also mention some of the people you are interested in by name, and give you a feeling for the period and suggestions as to what people considered important. Obituaries give information about the life of the individual (only as good as the source that provided it) and the names of the surviving relatives.

Get all your materials together and organized so you can spend your time productively. Take your notebook and charts, but leave your folders at home. Never carry originals or the only copies of your work with you. As you are working, keep records of where you didn't find material as well as where you did. This may save going over the same material twice.

Before going to the courthouse or the large genealogical libraries, practice your searching technique in your local library. The material you look up doesn't have to be about your family, but you may be delighted with what you find. You may discover that the library has archives, local history materials, and special collections of information that are separately listed. Librarians and record custodians work with their material every day and can often give you useful information on how to proceed. Accept their suggestions gracefully when they are given. They are less patient with pompous individuals who bark orders or start on long-winded tales of remote ancestors.

25

There are over 250 genealogical branch libraries maintained by the Church of Jesus Christ of Latter-Day Saints (Mormons) in the United States. These libraries are branches of the main LDS library in Salt Lake City, Utah, which is the largest genealogical library in the world. For information on the branch closest to you, call the Church in your area or write: Branch Libraries, LDS Church Office Building, Salt Lake City, Utah 84150. The branch libraries are run by knowledgeable volunteers and contain reference materials (mostly microfilm and microfiche). While the arrangements of the various libraries differ due to their physical facilities and geographical location, they all contain the same collection of basic reference material and catalogs from which materials can be ordered.

The Locality Catalog — If, for example, you are looking for material from DuPage County, Illinois, look under *Area*: North America; *Country*: United States; *State*: Illinois; *County*: DuPage.

After the locality, the information is broken down under the following headings: Atlas, Biography, Cemetery, Census, Church, Directories, Genealogy, History, Land and Property, Military, Newspapers, Probate, Taxes, Vital Records (birth, marriages, and deaths).

For each state, the information is given first for the state as a whole: Illinois — atlas; Illinois — biography, and so on. When the list of the categories is completed, then the same breakdown is gone through for each county in the state alphabetically. For example, Illinois, DuPage — atlas; Illinois, DuPage — biography. Information on foreign countries is handled in the same way, with the general information on the country coming first, and then the information on districts, states, or provinces.

Surname Catalog — This catalogue is arranged by family name and gives information on books or microfilms that the genealogical department has on a particular family.

Public records or documents are the property of the state or other political subdivision and are not the property of the individual who happens to have them in his custody. Unless the records have been closed to public inspection by a state or other government rule, one individual cannot suddenly decide to forbid the public to look at the records in his custody.

The hours which county and local offices are open often vary with the season and the community. Before you go, find out their hours and restrictions and plan your arrival time. Don't expect a warm welcome if you arrive on a Friday afternoon or 15 minutes before closing time.

Closing hours, even within a particular state, are quite individual, but if you have made a special trip and find the courthouse closed, don't feel the time is completely wasted. The history room of the library or historical society may have indexed many of the vital records as a Bicentennial project.

There are still places where women wearing pantsuits are not permitted, but you should dress comfortably (in layers) so that you can deal with either the sweating confines of an airless room or the freezing cold of poor insulation or modern air conditioning. Wear comfortable shoes that can take hard floors and narrow winding staircases.

Anyone using original or other public records should be aware of their responsibility and not deface them by removing portions or making changes. When you see something in records you feel or know or can prove is wrong, do *not* change it. If you feel strongly, write out your information on a separate sheet and give it to the person in charge who may decide to have it attached to the record. Remember that records should be handled very carefully.

Records on Microfilm and Microfiche

Many records are now available on microfilm and microfiche. They are often available through your library on interlibrary loan for a small fee. Make sure your library has a reader before you order.

On microfilm, the records have been copied on long rolls of film, and on microfiche, the records appear on

St. Louis, Missouri 1930

individual cards which may contain many pages of text. In either case, you have to use a machine to enlarge the image on the film before you can read it. Since there are so many different kinds of readers, it always saves time to get instructions on how the machine you are to use operates. In some libraries or archives there may be several different kinds of machines. There may even be a reader printer which can not only enlarge text but can also provide you with a copy you can keep.

When you locate the entry you are searching for, copy it all down, including the reference items to the roll or card. Keep each separate piece of information on separate pieces of paper or cards. You will find it easier to use later than if several pieces of information from separate sources are kept on the same sheet.

Religious Records

Religious records can be used to supplement or substitute for civil records, and in many parts of the country these records antedate the collection of civil records for birth, marriage, and death. One should keep in mind that the religious record may give the date of baptism or circumcision rather than the birth date and the date of burial rather than the date of death. While religious records can be extremely helpful, the difficulty is in locating them. They may have been lost or they may be found in the archives of an institution, in public libraries, or in private collections.

Many times there was only one church in town. Thus, when people moved they would change denominations. Their religious affiliation might also have changed with their social and economic situation. For example, an individual might be baptized an Episcopalian, marry as a Methodist, and die as a Presbyterian. Religious groups were not constant and often split or merged. Their buildings were often occupied by another denomination or converted to nonreligious use.

In one denomination the records belong to the congregation while in another they are the personal property of the minister. If you know that your ancestor belonged to a particular religious organization and it is still in existence, write or call and ask if the records are available and what the procedure is for searching them. The polite thing to do is to offer to pay for these services or to make a contribution.

Many religious organizations have archives or historical libraries but these often are devoted more to the personnel records of the ministers and the growth and disposition of property rather than information on the membership.

Two groups which have kept excellent records are the Society of Friends (Quakers) and the Church of Jesus Christ of Latter-Day Saints (Mormons). Friends were a relatively large proportion of the total population in the early 19th century and many families who have roots that go back to that period find that they have a "Friend" in the family. The outstanding record collector today is the Church of Jesus Christ of Latter-Day Saints whose members have copied every kind of civil and religious record throughout the world that might be used to develop family histories.

The National Archives

The National Archives are the depository for the permanent, legal, and administrative records of the federal government which have been considered worth saving from 1775 to the present. Not all records in the National Archives are available to the public. Generally, the records available from the Archives are the older records. The earliest records at the National Archives are the payrolls of soldiers serving in the Continental Army during the Revolutionary War and the Bounty Land Warrant files or pension files that resulted from the same service. Records prior to this time are usually found in those states which were colonies at the time of the Revolution, in Great Britain, or in other countries claiming land in what later became the United States.

The National Archives has regional branches located throughout the country. Each branch, in addition to basic records such as the U. S. census, contains federal records directly related to the area covered by the branch. Also, various branches may contain special collections such as the World War I Selective Service cards which are kept at the East Point, Georgia, center. Since the lists at each center are constantly being updated, it would be advisable to inquire if a record you are particularly interested in is available at the branch serving that area. A free kit containing forms to help you trace your family is available from the National Archives.

Land Records

"Putting down one's roots" is an expression associated with a degree of permanence and land ownership. Records, especially the earlier ones, frequently contain genealogical information. Land passed down from father to son might not appear in a courthouse record until it leaves the family. A man may have left no will but the distribution of his real estate in a land deed might mention his family.

In the United States land is described in two ways. In the East metes and bounds are used; that is, the boundary lines are defined with reference to a natural or artificial marker such as a tree, river, or stone. In the rest of the country, the rectangular survey system is used which was adopted at the time of the Northwest Ordinance of 1785. In this system land is surveyed and described in terms of rectangular sections, townships, and ranges.

Land records are indexed by a variety of methods. The legal description of property on a current tax bill identifies its location on the survey map. This same legal description is necessary to locate land purchases through the General Land Offices of the United States Government.

The indexes most often used to locate a land record

Chicago, Illinois 1905

when the legal description is not known are the grantor (seller) and the grantee (buyer) books located in each county courthouse. These show the seller or the buyer, when the transaction took place, and where the record can be found.

Not everyone completed his purchase. Procedures have changed very little over the past 200 years and mortgage books contain all kinds of information about those who "almost owned it."

When the buyer or seller lived in a place other than in the county where the land is located, their places of residence would usually be given. Because of the various indexes and systems used, it is always advisable to ask a records clerk to explain their procedures.

Before the Revolutionary War, records were filed in the counties or towns of the colonies, but after that date, as people migrated westward, buying and selling land originally held by the government was recorded in both the county (as it existed at that time) and in the General Land Office or both. Records of the former General Land Office are now in the National Archives.

Of particular interest to anyone searching the federal land records are *Preliminary Inventory of Land-Entry Papers of the General Land Office, PI-#22* and *List of Cartographic Records of the General Land Office* compiled by Laura E. Kelsay and available from the National Archives.

Towns are not always townships and the land township is not always the same as a civil township. Ask the record clerk where you can purchase a county highway map or a county township map. To become familiar with topographical features of the area, check an *Index to the Topographical Map for* [the particular state you are searching]. This state index can be requested without charge from the Branch of Distribution, U. S. Geological Survey Service. Using this index, you can order a quadrant map of your locality which will show roads, houses, cemeteries, churches, rivers, and other features. The order form is included with the index.

Indian Records

Records of the Indian peoples were kept by the War Department as early as 1789. The Bureau of Indian Affairs was not created until March 11, 1824. Since 1849, the Bureau has been a division of the Department of the Interior and directly responsible for all matters between the federal government and the Indian peoples.

The records of both the National Archives and the Bureau of Indian Affairs are varied. Bounty land warrant applications after the Revolutionary War are filed alphabetically, including a file of the tribal name, military organization, and dates of service. Estate files and heirship are indexed between 1910 and 1946; the census records may list only the name of the head of the household or show the age, sex, place of original residence, and the members of the household. The records of the removal of the Indian people to western lands are dated between 1830 and 1852, and the annuity rolls cover the years from 1848 to 1940.

A bibliography showing the routes of exploration, location of tribes, military reservations, proposals for churches, railroads, canals, telephone lines, and highways can be obtained from National Archives.

Government Agencies and Publications

The National Archives, Publication Sales Branch (NEPS), GSA, Washington DC 20408
>The National Archives and its regional branches (located in major metropolitan areas across the country) contain government records open to the public. Free publications available on request include:
>>A genealogical kit with sample order forms;
>>*Genealogical Records in the National Archives;*
>>*Genealogical Sources Outside the National Archives;*
>>*Military Service Records in the National Archives of the United States.*

Superintendent of Documents, Government Printing Office, Washington DC 20402
>Many of the government publications listed in this book are available through the GPO or the GPO bookstores located in major metropolitan areas across the country. Some important references are:
>>*Guide to Genealogical Records in the National Archives,* by Meredith B. Colkert, Jr., and Frank E. Bridgers. Washington DC, National Archives, 1964.
>>*Where To Write for Birth and Death Records,* DHEW HRA 76-1142;
>>*Where To Write for Divorce Records,* DHEW HRA 76-1145;
>>*Where To Write for Marriage Records,* DHEW HRA 76-1144.

Reading and Reference Suggestions

Daughters of the American Revolution: *Is That Lineage Right?* Washington DC, DAR, 1958.

Greenwood, Val D.: *The Researcher's Guide to American Genealogy.* Baltimore, Genealogical Publishing Co., 1973.

Kirkham, E. Kay: *A Handy Guide to Record-Searching in the Larger Cities of the United States.* Logan, Utah, Everton Publishers, 1974.

Major Genealogical Record Sources in the United States: A Guide to Major Sources and Their Availability. Salt Lake City, Genealogical Society of the Church of Jesus Christ of Latter-Day Saints, 1967.

Rubincam, Milton, and Stephenson, Jean (eds.): *Genealogical Research: Methods and Sources,* 2 vols. Washington DC, American Society of Genealogists, 1971.

Stevenson, Noel C.: *Search and Research: The Researcher's Handbook: A Guide to Official Records and Library Sources for Investigators, Historians, Genealogists, and Librarians,* rev. ed. Salt Lake City, Deseret Book Co., 1973.

Wright, Norman E.: *Building an American Pedigree: A Study in Genealogy.* Provo, Utah, Brigham Young University Press, 1974.

Newspapers

Brigham, Clarence S.: *History and Bibliography of American Newspapers, 1690-1820,* 2 vols. Worcester, Massachusetts, American Antiquarian Society, 1947.

Additions and Corrections. Worcester, Massachusetts, American Antiquarian Society, 1961.

Gregory, Winifred (ed.): *American Newspapers, 1821-1936: A Union List of Files Available in the United States and Canada.* New York, H. W. Wilson Co., 1937.

Johnson, J., and Percy, H. (eds.): *N. W. Ayers & Sons Directory of Newspapers and Periodicals* (published annually).

Library of Congress: *Newspapers in Microform, United States, 1948-1972.* Library of Congress, 1973.

Check List of Foreign Newspapers in the Library of Congress. GPO, 1929.

Religious Records

Cache Genealogical Library: *Handbook for Genealogical Correspondence,* rev. ed. Logan, Utah, Everton Publishers, 1976.

Kirkham, E. Kay: *A Survey of American Church Records,* ed. 3. Logan, Utah, Everton Publishers, 1971.

Heiss, Willard: *Abstracts of the Records of the Society of Friends in Indiana.* Indianapolis, Indiana Historical Society, 1962—.

Hinshaw, William Wade (ed.): *Encyclopedia of American Quaker Genealogy,* 6 vols. Baltimore, Genealogical Publishing Co., 1936.

Rottenberg, Dan: *Finding Our Fathers: A Guidebook to Jewish Genealogy.* New York, Random House, 1977.

Stern, Malcolm H.: *Jewish Synagogue Records.* Salt Lake City, Genealogical Society of the Church of Jesus Christ of Latter-Day Saints, 1969.

Gone But Not Forgotten

A great deal of information can be gleaned from wills, cemetery records, death certificates, and obituaries. The splendid tombstones favored by earlier generations can tell you a lot about birthplaces, marriages, occupations, and children as well as dates of birth and death.

Chicago, Illinois 1920

Chicago, Illinois 1902

How do you prove that a person has died rather than moved elsewhere and started a new life? The most obvious answer is the death certificate. The disposition of the body is included in religious records, usually recorded at a later date. The mortician or funeral director will keep a record, as will the cemetery office or the department or organization responsible for burials. The stonecutter will have a record. A notice may appear in local papers or the paper of a church, social, fraternal, or patriotic organization. For the past 40 years, if the deceased was over 65, Social Security has been notified, in addition to his/her insurance company. If the body was taken from one state to another, the death certificate was recorded in the first state and a permit for burial in the second. Local libraries and historical societies may keep a card file of individuals buried in a particular cemetery.

Chicago, Illinois 1900

The records of a death can appear in many places but they may not all say the same thing. The death certificate contains name, date and place of birth, and the cause of death, as well as the name and birthplace of the father and the mother, the names of the informant and mortician, and the place of burial. Consider the conditions and pressures under which the above information was given as well as the closeness of the relationship of the two people. A grandson or a neighbor tell what they believe is true and the clerk writes down what he assumes is true. For example, a clerk entered the name of the informant (who was not a member of the family) as the surname of a deceased married woman. The record was filed under the informant's name and the error was only discovered 40 years after the woman's death.

Obituary notices in the newspaper are excellent potential sources of information. They sometimes include a short biography with age and former residence, marital status, names of relatives and heirs and their residences, social and fraternal affiliations, and the name of the undertaker and place of burial. The amount of information given will vary according to the custom of each community.

The National Archives and the Adjutant General's office keep a record of burials in the national cemeteries and the records (since 1792) of the deaths of civilian Americans in foreign countries. This record may consist of an obituary, the inventory of an estate, or a court record. The files from 1857 to 1922 are indexed.

Mortality census schedules taken in 1850, 1860, 1870, and 1880 record the name and cause of death of each person dying in the year preceding June of the census year. The 1880 mortality schedules also include the birthplaces of the individual and his parents.

Each year the Daughters of the American Revolution report to Congress on the graves of Revolutionary soldiers which have been identified. The reports, published annually, are found in the larger libraries.

Cemetery Records

Because a tombstone is in a particular cemetery doesn't necessarily prove the individual is buried under it unless you also have access to the actual interment record. The information on the interment record is usually copied from the religious or civil order for burial or the mortician's note, and this information is only as accurate as the personal knowledge and mental condition of the person who gave it at the time arrangements for the burial were being made.

Tombstones have crumbled, been broken by vandals, been removed to build patios, and deliberately destroyed for religious reasons. Tombstones have been erected and re-erected years later by loving descendants or admiring patriots. Because a cemetery is located next to what was once a church does not mean its use was restricted to members of that church. Some families were buried in special plots on their own farms. If you want to check these, you need permission of the owner and an assurance that the bulls are in a different pasture.

Most people don't visit old cemeteries just to look at the tombstones. They also read the inscriptions and absorb the history, symbolism, and humor of the stonecutter's art.

Cemetery searching requires definite equipment and dress. Wear something with long sleeves, heavy pants, and boots to protect you from stinging, creeping, crawling, catching, and slithering objects. Use a sickle to remove tall grasses and weeds around the stones. While a lawnmower might be easier, it is considerably less portable. When you have identified the stone you are looking for, take a block of Styrofoam and clean off any lichens or moss. Use a piece of chalk to highlight (but not alter) the letters and numerals. Take a picture or two. If the light is bad or you have run out of film, you can place a piece of butcher's paper over the stone and make a rubbing with the flat side of a crayon or a carpenter's pencil. In your notebook write down the date of your visit, the location of the cemetery, the approximate position of the tombstone, and exactly what is inscribed on it. The numerals 1, 4, and 7, 5 and 6, or 3 and 8 can be confused. Whenever there is any doubt about part of an inscription, make a square bracket around the doubtful portion. The rubbing will sometimes reveal the true figures. Write down the information from the adjacent tombstones — people buried under them may be relatives — and sketch the shape and design of the stone. The patterns used migrated with the people and may provide further clues. If you see the finger pointing heavenward, you've probably spotted a Methodist!

Read some of the other tombstone inscriptions before it gets too dark:

A Pale consumption gave the fatal blow!
The stroke was certain but the effect was slow,
With wasting pain death found me long oppressed
Pitied my sighs & kindly brought me rest.
                              or
Behold and See as you pass by
As you are now so once was I
As I am now you soon will be
Prepare for death and follow me.

For 83 years members of the DAR have been copying cemetery records and depositing one copy in their library in Washington, DC, and another in a designated library in their respective states.

When you find a stone inscribed with the date of death and the person's age you can subtract and get the approximate date of birth. Even if your subtraction is right, the answer may be wrong because individuals were often fuzzy in keeping track of their age.

Probate Records

Probate records refer to the assortment of documents which complete the process of settling the real and personal estate of a dead (or incompetent) person. Where they exist, they are one of the most important series of documents to identify one or more generations of a family.

The court where the documents are recorded (located in the county or probate district) is called by various names: Surrogate Court, Orphans Court, Court of Probate, Ordinary Court, or Prefect Court.

Whether the individual has made a nuncupative (oral, deathbed) will, left a lengthy written one, or no will at all, the deceased's affairs must be put in order. Minor children have guardians appointed, notice is given to any creditors who wish to make a claim, and all heirs are located. An inventory is ordered and the list, with the value of each item, is presented to the court. Carpentry tools, farming implements, or physician's books provide clues to the deceased person's occupation.

In earlier wills, relations posted the bond. One executor was the husband's relative and the other the wife's. The movable, personal property was usually given to the daughters and the land to the sons. The oldest usually got a larger portion. If the property was divided into sevenths, there were probably six heirs, with the oldest getting a double portion. The distribution of the estate and the release signed by the heirs are as important as the will itself since they name the wife, the sons and the daughters, including their married names, and current residences.

Was the stated residence at the time the will was written in the same county where it was offered for probate or did the individual move, either at the time the will was written or before the estate was distributed? Had a child died and were grandchildren named to receive their parent's portion?

Whenever possible it is advisable to read the original or a microfilm or photocopy of a will and all related documents. Abstracts (some have been published) usually hit the high spots and might leave out the very facts you are searching for.

An abstract of a probate record should include: (1) the state, county, or probate district where the record was found; (2) the name and location of the court; (3) the book, page, or file number for locating all documents (wills are usually indexed in this manner); (4) the name of the deceased, date of death, date the will was written, residence at the time it was written, and the date the will was entered into probate; (5) the date when the estate was distributed, to whom, and their residences; and (6) the names of witnesses, executors, and bondsmen.

Reading and Reference Suggestions

Jones, Mary-Ellen: *Photographing Tombstones: Equipment and Techniques,* technical leaflet 92. Nashville, American Association of State and Local History, 1977.

Newman, John J.: *Cemetery Transcribing: Preparation and Procedure,* technical leaflet 9. Nashville, American Association of State and Local History, 1971.

Military Records and Benefits

The military has kept files on its personnel for generations. Some of these records go back to the French and Indian Wars before the Revolution. It is vital information that can help you learn rank and length of service, names of dependents, and the birthplaces, and physical appearance of many of your ancestors.

Parris Island, South Carolina 1950

Russia, 1913

Washington 1918

Over the past 200 years, the United States has engaged in a surprising number of wars. About 10 percent of today's population has seen military service. The personal information in the early records may be sparse, but later records, especially those dealing with veterans' benefits, can be filled with family information.

Military service records from 1607 to 1774 are located in the archives of the colonies (states), towns, or Great Britain. This includes service in King William's War (1690-1697), Queen Anne's War (1702-1713), King George's War (1744-1748), and the French and Indian War (1754-1763). Many of these records have been published and are available in state archives or state libraries, in historical societies, or in the genealogical collection of the larger libraries. The records for the American Revolution Militia Service (1775-1783) may be found in the states.

Service Records

For those who wish to do their own research on the military service records of the Revolutionary War, microfilm rolls are available on interlibrary loan from the National Archives or federal record centers.

Microcopy T 515, the general index to the compiled military service records of Revolutionary War soldiers, is arranged alphabetically by surname, so be sure to state the full name of the serviceman and any other spelling variations. Microcopy 246, roll 1, provides the index to the rolls which list the particular troops in alphabetical sequence and gives the jacket number where the remaining information is located.

The National Archives contains the records of those who served in the numerous domestic and foreign wars prior to 1900. These conflicts include the War Against the Northwest Indians (Wayne's War, 1790-1795), the Whiskey Insurrection (or Rebellion; 1794), the War of 1812 (1812-1815), the Black Hawk War (against the Sac and Fox Indians, 1831-1832), the Civil War (Union and Confederate records, 1861-1865), the Spanish American War (1898), and the Philippine Insurrection (including the records of the Puerto Rico Regiment of U.S. Volunteers; 1899-1901).

Navy and Marine records prior to 1896 and Army records from 1774 until well into the 20th century (October 31, 1912, for enlisted personnel and June 30, 1917, for officers) are available from the National Archives.

If World War I records are not available, and the

Camp Lewis, Washington 1918

Missouri 1917

Korea 1951

individual you are interested in would have been of an age eligible for military service in 1918, you can write to the Federal Records Center located at East Point, Georgia, where a card index for every man of draft age in the United States in 1918 is kept. This information is available for a fee. Information given includes birthplace, age, residence, next of kin, and marital status.

The length and type of service will be shown in the various records — pay vouchers, military orders from 1797 to 1939, Civil War draft records from 1863 to 1866, military prisons and medical records, military reservations, and special ethnic group materials such as *The Negro in the Military Service of the United States* (an eight-volume compilation of copies of official records, state papers, and historical facts relating to military service and status from colonial times through the Civil War arranged chronologically) and *Descriptive Lists of Colored Volunteers 1864* (a 54-volume compilation arranged chronologically, with each volume indexed by name, containing descriptive lists of black volunteers enlisted in the Army under General Order #135, November 14, 1863, giving name, age, color of eyes, hair, complexion, height, place of birth, occupation, date of enlistment, by whom and for what period, and, if a former slave, owner's name).

Each war produces its own records. Military service records, whether in national or state archives, prove an individual served in some capacity. Not all military service records contain the same information. Many files for the Revolutionary War show only that an individual was present and accounted for when the roll call was taken, while an enlistment record for the Civil War might include date and place of birth, color of hair and eyes, and, even height.

Bounty Land Records

From 1776 to 1855 free land from the public domain was a form of benefit that was given to veterans or their heirs for military service performed.

The first public land grant in 1776 provided for officers or soldiers in the service who remained until the end of the Revolutionary War (or to the representatives of officers and soldiers slain by the enemy). The land was granted according to rank. Colonels were to get 500 acres, lieutenant colonels 450 acres, on down to 100 acres per soldier. The expense of providing the land was to be borne by the individual states.

This was very unsatisfactory, and in 1787 a specific tract of land, known as the Military District, was set aside to supply land grants and end piecemeal distribution. Initially a veteran had to accept his bonus in this area, but by 1856 he or his heirs could choose a location reaching further westward to Arkansas, Illinois, or Missouri.

As soldiers and sailors who had served for 14 days or more in the American Revolution, the War of 1812, the Indian Wars, or the Mexican War migrated westward with their families, towns and villages were created and the feeling of security brought even more people. Local governments were established in the new territories, states were formed, and industries followed as need arose.

The bounty warrant application files, the documents relating to claims for land based on military service, include a warrant application, veteran's discharge, certificate to substantiate the claim, and a notation as to whether or not the claim was approved. Some individuals who received bounty land sold their rights to the land rather than move to the frontier.

Pension Records

The first U. S. military pension law, passed in 1792, provided aid to disabled veterans who had served in the Revolutionary War; later pensions were extended to anyone who had served. In 1818, a veteran had to prove actual need; in 1820, a veteran had to prove need and submit a schedule of his estate, perhaps a copy of a deed showing that he had disposed of all his property. All veterans were granted pensions after 1828.

The U. S. Government paid about $70,000,000 in pensions for the Revolutionary War, $46 million for the War of 1812, $62 million for the Mexican War, and payment to Civil War veterans and their dependents was over $8 billion. Useful family information can be found in the pension application files.

The more recent the records, the greater the amount of family information that can be extracted from them. Pension files are the most important military record for the family historian since they include claims, affidavits, letters, and back-up material to support those claims. Service files do not contain much family information.

The usual procedure for initiating an early pension claim was for the veteran or his dependents to go before a court of record in his county and present evidence that would prove that the service had been given. In a veteran's application, the most important information available is the period of service, age, and place of birth. When a widow was applying, additional information would include place and date of marriage.

The 1836 Widows' Act provided that the widow of a Revolutionary War veteran could claim his pension. The widow had to prove relationship and establish that they had been married before the war ended. After 1854 widows were eligible for a pension regardless of the date of the marriage. However, many who were eligible did not apply.

An interesting file is the Remarried Widows' Index which is arranged alphabetically by the name of the remarried widow. Part I covers 1861 and before and Part II covers the period from the Civil War to World War I. Information on the card includes name of remarried widow, name of veteran, the unit he served in, and his file or certificate number.

When a widow claimed a pension on behalf of a minor child, she also included proof of the child's age and date of birth.

In 1969, as part of the Bicentennial celebration, the National Archives started microfilming these records to make them more available and to protect the originals. They combined all related papers into a single file in the same claim folder.

Military Records in Government Files

Revolutionary War: General Index to Compiled Military Service Records of Revolutionary War Soldiers (National Archives microfilm).

Army: Records for officers from 1789 to 1916 and enlisted men from 1789 to 1912 are in the National Archives (GSA Form 6751). Queries about personnel separated after these dates should be sent to Military Personnel Records, GSA, 9700 Page Blvd., St. Louis, Missouri 63132 (Standard Form 180).

Navy and Marine Corps: Navy and Marine service records for the Revolutionary War (1775-1783) and for the Confederate States (1861-1865), naval officers from 1798 to 1902 and enlisted men from 1798 to 1885, and Marine Corps personnel from 1798 to 1895 are in the National Archives. GSA Form 6751 should be used only for queries about Revolutionary and Confederate service records. Other requests should be made by letter. Queries about personnel separated after these dates should be sent to Military Personnel Records, GSA, 9700 Page Blvd., St. Louis, Missouri 63132.

Note: All service records less than 75 years old are subject to restrictions imposed by the Department of Defense.

Pension and Bounty Land Applications: Pension applications based on service between 1775 and 1916 and bounty land applications based on service between 1775 and 1855 are in the National Archives (GSA Form 6751).

Reading and Reference Suggestions

Daughters of the American Revolution: *The Patriots Index.* Washington DC, DAR, 1966; supplements published, 1969, 1973, 1976.

Groene, Bertram H.: *Tracing Your Civil War Ancestor.* Winston-Salem, North Carolina, John F. Blair, 1973.

Hoyt, Max Ellsworth: *Index of Revolutionary War Pension Applications.* Washington DC, National Genealogical Society, 1966, and later supplements.

Where Did They Come From?

The millions of immigrants who came to this land left records behind. Ship passenger lists, immigration records, and naturalization papers are clues to your family's origin. These valuable sources of documentary evidence make it easier to discover where your people came from.

Chicago, Illinois 1910

Chicago, Illinois 1915

Chicago, Illinois 1840

Poland 1930

LaSalle, Illinois 1910

Where did your family really come from? Have you the foggiest idea? We are a nation of immigrants.

Immigration

In the 18th century there was a continuous call for labor in the colonies. Land was rich but the number who could work it were few. The need was answered by convict labor, indentured servants, and slaves. The prisoners transported from England found themselves in Maryland, Virginia, and Georgia. From 1737 to 1767, 20,000 convicts were sent to Maryland alone. As the number became a problem, the Crown, in response to the complaints of the wealthy landowners, sent prisoners to Botany Bay, Australia. The transporters kept good records, indicating the name of the prisoner, the ship and sailing date, and that the guaranteed confinement had been enforced.

Individuals desiring passage to this country but without sufficient funds would "sell" themselves for a certain period of time as indentured servants, working without pay in return for passage money, food, clothing, and shelter. At the end of their period of service, they were supposed to be given a new suit of clothes and equipped with an axe or hoe, and often a grant of

land from the colonial government. Practices varied in the different colonies.

In 1619, the first blacks arrived in Virginia as indentured servants. By 1688, when the Quakers issued their first anti-slavery protest, black slavery was well established.

Although several of the states had their own immigration laws between 1830 and 1875 which restricted immigration by individuals who might become public charges, federal regulation of immigration began in 1875. Immigration controls began in 1882 when the United States passed its first general immigration statute which excluded the insane, convicts, and people likely to become public charges. In 1882, three of every four immigrants were from northern and western Europe. By 1896, one half were from southern and eastern Europe, and in the early 1900's seven of every ten were from southern and eastern Europe. The quota laws of 1921 and 1924 and the National Origins Act of 1929 were designed to slow down immigration.

Records were not kept of overland arrivals from Mexico or Canada. But ship captains have been required since 1819 to give the government a list including the name, age, sex, occupation, date of arrival in

Naturalization

Naturalization is the legal process by which a person changes his citizenship from one country to another.

During the Colonial period, citizenship was a natural thing for British subjects or individuals born in the colonies. The colonial government required allegiance to the British Crown, but individuals were citizens of a particular colony. In the late 1600's non-English people took the oath of allegiance to a particular colony so that they might buy land from the Indians and so that their children would not have any trouble when they come to inherit it.

In 1740, Parliament passed a law requiring a seven-year residence in a colony before an oath could be taken renouncing allegiance to a previous sovereign. One of the requirements for naturalization was that the name given must be a true one, but this didn't mean that the name had to be spelled in the same way that it appeared on other documents.

Originally, each state handled its own unique naturalization procedure, but in 1790 the federal government passed legislation for uniform naturalization procedures that made white males citizens of every state. The period of waiting time between arrival and application for citizenship varied from two to fourteen years. In 1801, the waiting time was set at five years, the period required today. After 1802, the applicant had to prove that he had entered the country legally and many application forms give information as to the date of arrival and the port of entry. Although the specific place of origin may sometimes appear on the form, it often lists only the country, the largest city near by, or the port from which the boat departed.

The Bureau of Immigration and Naturalization was established in 1906. Information on immigration and naturalization since that time is available from the Immigration and Naturalization Service. After 1906, the naturalization procedure became more complex. First an immigrant had to fill out an application, "first papers," which asked for detailed information. Then this information was checked out by the nearest federal court and, if the results of the investigation were favorable and the proper length of time had passed, the certificate was granted.

For searches of the naturalization records after April 1, 1956, requests should be made on Form N-585 to the Office of Naturalization and Immigration nearest to the place where the individual lived. These offices can be found in the telephone book listed under United States Government, Justice Department — Immigration and Naturalization Service. For dates between April 1, 1956, and September 17, 1906, Form N-585 should be sent directly to the Immigration and Naturalization Service. Records are also maintained in the court in which the person was naturalized and may be obtained directly from the clerk of that court. The courts are the sources for records before 1906.

America, and the port from which they sailed, for all passengers carried.

New York was not the only port of entry for people coming into the United States. Ocean steamers came in at such other places as Bridgeport and Hartford, Connecticut, Oswegatchie and Rochester, New York, or Sandusky, Ohio. Olga Miller in her book, *Migration, Emigration and Immigration,* has a four-page list of ports where people might have entered, with dates of the available records. Most of the records for the West Coast ports are missing. The San Francisco records were burned in the fires of 1851 and 1940 and many of the others cannot be found.

Passengers lists from the present back to 1891 (1897 for New York) are available from the Immigration and Naturalization Service on Form N-585. From 1891 back to 1820, records are available from the National Archives on Form GSA 7111. You send no money but are billed if and when something is found.

Passenger lists before 1820 are available in the port of entry or the state archives of the state in which the port is located. Using immigration records is not easy and can be frustrating, but sometimes they can be a great help in establishing the place from which a member of your family originally came.

Poland 1910

LaSalle, Illinois 1907

Migration

Land was a magnet in the developing United States. The word of available land spread quickly to the many people in Europe where hope for survival was slim and much land was held by the few. On this side of the ocean there was more political and religious freedom, and cheap and readily available land. Anyone willing to work hard could build a home on his own land. As a further inducement to migration, there were individuals in America who were paying the passage of passengers from Europe in return for a "headright grant" of 50 acres multiplied by the number of people they brought over.

Land was offered free and for sale for as little as 33½ cents an acre. The land could be paid for in full or on extended credit. The location of the land and terms all varied but the transfer records are filled with information. The records involving the federal government are available both through the regional branches of the National Archives and in the area where the land is located. In 1841, a widow of a veteran, an American citizen, or anyone who had declared his intention of becoming an American citizen could purchase 160 acres for $1.25 per acre.

Land that had been on the market for 30 years or

more was offered for 12½ cents an acre in 1850. At the same time, anyone married or single who could be induced to go to the east coast of Florida or to New Mexico, Oregon, or Washington territories to protect the government's interests could acquire 160 to 640 acres of free land — donation land as it was called. With the Homestead Act of 1862, a potential settler, for just a small filing fee, could apply for 160 free acres. After he had lived on it for five years, cultivated it, and built his home, he could apply for title. Citizenship or application for it was another requirement. The Union Army and Navy veterans of the Civil War were considered to have automatically met the requirement, but by 1872, all Civil War veterans with 90 days or more of service could apply up to four years of their service to the usual five-year residency requirement.

Ten percent of the new farms between 1862 and 1892 were acquired under homesteading. The good land was usually bought from the railroads or the people who knew where the railroads were going to go. The grants to the railroads gave them land adjacent to their right of way. They sold this land to provide capital for building and many people preferred to get land which was close to transportation. In addition, the railroads often provided agricultural advice and extended credit.

By 1850, the first tier of states west of the Mississippi was populated and by 1890, the population moving west from the Mississippi started to meet the population moving east from the West Coast. In 1890, people could no longer improve their condition by going west, so they started moving into the cities where industry was providing new opportunity. Urbanization has also been accelerated by two World Wars and changing occupation patterns.

Where To Start

Remember that the further people are from home, the more general will be the territorial designation of the place they have come from.

Many families that arrived from one of the German states before World War I were later quiet about their German parentage, and when asked vaguely referred to Holland, France, Switzerland, Czechoslovakia, or Poland.

Where do you start? Family traditions are important and can give you a place to start, but they have to be checked and verified. Do you have any pictures or letters? A photograph might have a name and address on it. If the picture is in a frame, check and see if anything is written on the back. Are there any old letters? If they are still in their envelope with a stamp and postmark that you can read, you're in great luck. These are not only valuable within the United States; but can also give a clue to national origins. What language is the letter written in? If you can't read it, check with your local librarians. They can often help you determine the language, and then you can look for a friend, neighbor, fraternal organization, or consulate that can give you a hand. Old letters are great sources of information and fun to read. Does it contain news of other members of the family?

Do you have naturalization papers or an application for naturalization? On the papers, a statement is made renouncing allegiance to the previous country, where the individual entered the United States, and, if you are lucky, you may get the name of a home town rather than the port sailed from. Have you checked the census? Starting with the 1880 census, a column was included for the birthplaces of the parents of each individual as well as the birthplace of the individual himself.

What were the usual routes taken? People usually traveled together in a group or went the "best way" which had been established first by the buffalo, then by the Indians, and finally by the settlers.

If you know the time period in which your family traveled, you can usually find a map showing the route they took.

The form of transportation depended on the period. If they were traveling in the 18th century, it was by foot, horse, carriage, wagon train, or boat. In the 20th century, the automobile and airplane have speeded up transportation even more and made it possible for more people to go further distances.

Immigration and Naturalization Records in the National Archives

Naturalization
From 1787 to 1906: Photocopies of records from Maine, Massachusetts, New Hampshire, and Rhode Island are available in the National Archives. Inquiries for other states must be made to the clerk of the court that issued the naturalization certificate.
After September 16, 1906: Inquiries should be directed to Immigration and Naturalization Service, Washington DC 20536 (obtain Form N-585 from any district office of the Service).

Passenger Lists
Prior to 1926: Incomplete records are available in the National Archives. Other records may be available at the port of entry.
After 1927: Records are not open to the public.

Reading and Reference Suggestions

Miller, Olga: *Migration, Emigration, and Immigration.* Logan, Utah, Everton Publishers, 1974.

Pine, Leslie G.: *American Origins: A Handbook of Genealogical Sources Throughout Europe.* Garden City, New York, Doubleday, 1960.

Stevenson, J. Grant: *Research Aids for the British Isles, Continental Europe, United States and Canada,* ed. 2. Salt Lake City, Utah, Genealogical Society, 1962.

Wellauer, Marilyn A.: *A Guide to Foreign Genealogical Research.* Milwaukee, privately printed, 1976.

Bouncing Boundaries

Boundary lines are far from stable. State, county, and national boundaries change with time. In addition, major historical events such as the Russian Revolution or the emancipation of colonies often meant renaming cities and towns.

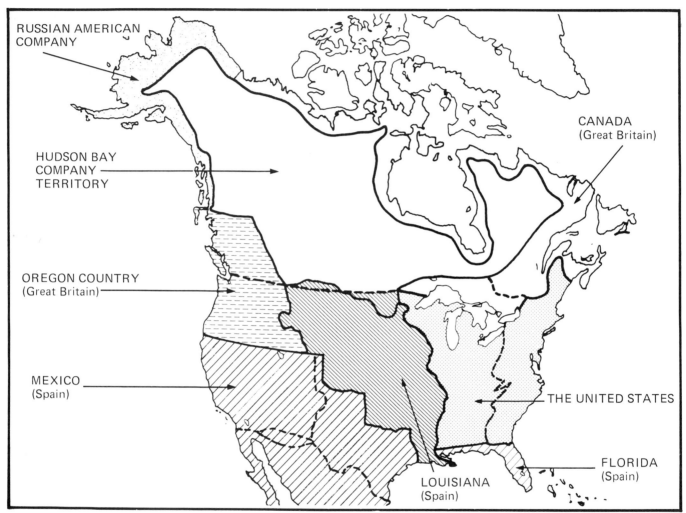

North America 1800

Boundaries are natural or arbitrary limits used to define the limits of jurisdiction of a city, county, state, or country. Although definite, they are not permanent. At any one time it is possible for two or more jurisdictions to disagree on a boundary's exact location.

Natural boundaries change when the river moves or the bay fills up. Political boundaries are even more changeable since they are imaginary lines that everyone does not necessarily agree to. Boundaries are very elastic. They move about, especially in times of war or when there are large migrations of people.

When looking for people in the records, establishing the boundaries at the time the record was made is very important, since where a person lived or where his property was located determines where his record is to be found.

At the time of the American Revolution, modern Kentucky, West Virginia, and much of Ohio were part of Virginia. Tennessee was part of North Carolina (which claimed a strip of land all the way to the

Pacific). Maine was in Massachusetts and Vermont was an independent state that was claimed by both New York and New Hampshire. Much of the territory claimed by these states was also being claimed by England, France, and Spain. The dates when the states or territories were formed and the sources of their land can be found in many standard reference books.

The date of organization into a territory is useful since territorial papers may be among the territorial papers in the National Archives or in the state library or the state archives, or scattered among them.

In the states the vital statistics records are usually kept at the state capital with additional copies available at the city, town, or county office. Land records are found in the county as are the probate records in most states. (However, in the following states the probate district and the county do not have the same boundaries: Arkansas, Connecticut, Indiana, Iowa, Massachusetts, Mississippi, Montana, Nevada, North Carolina, Rhode Island, Utah, Vermont, and Wyoming.)

It is possible that a family that lived in one spot for a long time has records scattered over a number of different counties, because the county's boundaries have changed a number of times. For example, when Ohio was admitted into the Union in 1803, it contained many fewer counties than it does today. On the east and on the south there were small populated counties and the rest of the counties were very large. As the population increased, the original counties were divided many times. An example of this is Cook County, Illinois. Cook County was formed from Putnam County in 1831 which was formed from Fulton County (1825), which was formed from Pike County (1823), which was formed from Clark County (1821), which was formed from Crawford County (1819), which was formed from Edwards County (1816), which was formed from Gallatin County (1814), which was formed from Randolph County (1812), which was founded in 1795 from the Northwest Territory.

Sometimes deciding where the record might be takes longer than finding it. *The Handy Book for Genealogists* is very useful in giving the histories of the counties' formation and in providing current county maps for each state. County histories, local directories, and maps of the period are useful in tracking down communities. Maps that were made at the same time as the record you are searching are very useful in identifying the location of a town that may no longer be in existence, may have had its name changed, or may have been incorporated into a larger town nearby. Contemporary maps are especially important when searching the census records before 1880. It can save a great deal of time if you have the township or ward and don't have to search a larger area. If you have the name of the town and you are not sure where it is located, you can start with a gazetteer or post office directory. If you have the area, get a U.S. Geological Survey topographical map. It will be a big help since the terrain will determine how people

moved about. In the early days it was easier to float down a river than to climb a mountain and easier to stay on one side of the river (if there was no ferry or bridge) than to cross it. A mountain or a river might slow people down but an imaginary line — a jurisdictional boundary — would not. People did business, went to church, and were buried in the more convenient location and they didn't care whether it was located in the same county, state, or country.

In addition to the *Handy Book for Genealogists* you may want to consult one or more of the books listed here for specific information on boundaries and the development of counties.

One thing to watch out for when working with a county that had just been organized is the fact that states sometimes created a county before there were many people to live in it, and a number of counties were slow to start recording and filing information.

Even if a boundary did not change, the name of the town or area may have. Parks in some towns have been renamed three times to honor new individuals. Streets can be renamed with the new name completely replacing the old — such as Keyser Avenue being changed to Wilson Avenue during World War I. Sometimes both names continue to be used at the same time — such as the Eisenhower (Congress) Expressway in Chicago. Bouncing boundaries are not found only in the United States, but in all parts of the world. Since most people in the United States originally came from Europe, *An Atlas of European History* can be a big help. This book, which is available in paperback, gives you a good idea of the changing national boundaries in Europe.

Reading and Reference Suggestions

Everton, George B., and Rasmuson, Gunnar: *The Handy Book for Genealogists,* ed. 6. Logan, Utah, Everton Publishers, 1971.

Fox, Richard Whiting: *An Atlas of European History.* New York, Oxford University Press, 1957.

Index to the Topographical Map for [insert name of state]. Branch of Distribution, U.S. Geological Survey Service, 1200 S. Eads St., Arlington, Virginia.

Kirkham, E. Kay: *The Counties of the United States and Their Genealogical Value.* Salt Lake City, Deseret Book Co., 1964.

Library of Congress, Map Division: *A List of Geographical Atlases in the Library of Congress.* Reprinted, New York, Paladin Press, 1968.

Peterson, Clarence Stewart: *Consolidated Bibliography of County Histories in Fifty States in 1961.* Baltimore, Genealogical Publishing Co., 1973.

Stephenson, Richard W.: *Land Ownership Maps: A Checklist of Nineteenth Century United States County Maps in the Library of Congress.* Washington DC, Superintendent of Documents, 1967.

Van Zandt, Franklin K.: *Boundaries of the United States and the Several States.* Geological Survey Bulletin 1212.

Is the Name the Same?

People change their names for a variety of reasons. Immigrants often took new names that were easier to spell and pronounce than their original ones. Sometimes family names were translated into their English equivalents. The creative spelling of the past can also cause confusion.

Morris, Illinois 1895

Many times the first thing we know about a person is his name. In earlier times a name could sometimes give hints about an individual's background and interests. Most surnames originally had definite meanings. They might refer to an occupation such as smith. Each town had to have a smith and the French smiths were called Lefevre, the German ones Schmidt, the Italian Ferraro, the Arabic Haddad, and the Spanish Herrera. The same thing is true with other occupations — Zimmermann for a carpenter and Miller for a grinder of meal.

A large proportion of names are derived from the names of things such as property (Stonehouse, Newhouse, Furnace, Millhouse), colors (Black, White, Grey, Green, Brown), landscapes (Meadow, Park, Bridge, Forest, Garden, Wood, Lake), and birds (Swan, Dove).

People's names are not as stable as one might think, although within the past 50 years or so all the laws requiring the registration of births, deaths, and marriages, the proliferation of records such as Social Security, military, and drivers' licenses have tended to make names more stable. In some parts of the world the general use of permanent last names (surnames) is rather new. For example, it wasn't until 1901 that Swedish law established permanent family surnames. Most people decided to use their patronymic ("son of") name as a surname. This produced many people with the same last name — so many that in 1946 a Family Name Committee was set up to help people change their names. To assist the committee, a list of 50,000 new names was produced using a computer.

Originally a surname was an extra name, a nickname, or a name added for identification; it was not necessarily the family name. Patronymic names are very common in all languages. Some of the more common prefixes or suffixes are: Arabic, *Ibn;* Chinese, *Tse;* Danish, *sen;* English, *son;* French, *de;* German, *sohn* or *zohn;* Greek, *poulos;* Hebrew, *ben;* Irish, *Mac* (O' indicates grandson); Norman, *Fitz;* Polish, *wicz;* Russian, *ovich, na;* Spanish, *es, ez;* Welsh, *ap, s.*

The most common names used in the United States have not changed too much over the years. The nine most common names in the 1790 census in order of use were Smith, Brown, Davis, Jones, Johnson, Clark, Williams, Miller, and Wilson. In 1964 an examination of Social Security files found the top ten names to be in order of use: Smith, Johnson, Brown, Williams, Jones, Miller, Davis, Martin, Anderson, and Wilson.

To perpetuate a family name, a surname is sometimes used as a given name and can provide a clue to family connections. In many families there are certain given names that are used over and over again. The same given name might also be given to more than one child of the same sex in the same family to make sure that at least one child with that name would survive. When more than one survived it can make separating people a bit challenging. In German families it was often the custom to give all the boys their father's name and all the girls their mother's name. It was a compliment to the parents, but means that one has to be especially careful about the other names.

A number of immigrants had no surname when they came to the United States. Some of these adopted their patronymics. Some immigrants translated their names into English, others cut off prefixes, suffixes, or both, and others took, or were given, entirely different names. Some of these immigrants were known in their family by one name and in the English-speaking community by another.

In the 1890's there were people using two completely different names at the same time. Many Irish were simultaneously using Gaelic and English names, and different members of the same family might be using different names at the same time. This confusion started with a statute (1465) ordering the Irish to take English names or have their goods confiscated.

Anyone may establish a new name and signature merely by using it all the time, and most states permit an individual to change his name if no fraud is intended.

Much of the diversity in names is the result of spelling variations. Until fairly recently, people spelled names as they were pronounced and the same name might be spelled several ways in the same document. When looking for members of your family in public records keep this in mind and check under all possible spelling variations. A big help in making sure that you have most of them is to make a list of all the names under the Soundex code for your family name. Creative spelling could produce Furnace, Furnas, or Firness.

Among the principal reasons for changing names are: marriage, difficulties in spelling and pronunciation, making a clean break with the past, qualifying for an inheritance, going back to a name previously used (e.g., resumption of maiden name after divorce), and giving a child the same name as the mother's new husband; in addition, during a war or threat of war, many people change their names so there won't be questions about their allegiance.

When working with names other challenges are those that have to do with the sex of the individual bearing a name. For example, Beverly, Joyce, Shirley, Leslie, and Lynn have been used for both boys and girls. And then there are names not too frequently used today such as Waitstill, Experience, and Godsgift which can be equally puzzling.

The meaning of forms of address have changed too. Mrs., the abbreviation of Mistress, was used for unmarried women in the 17th and 18th centuries and Junior and Senior did not necessarily mean son and father, but were often applied to the younger and older of two people with the same name living in the same area. Forms of address that suggest relationships should be considered carefully before making assumptions. Brother and sister were not only used for offspring of the same parents but also for individuals with whom one felt a close relationship. These terms were also used in addressing members of religious groups. Mother and father, in addition to the obvious use, were sometimes used to identify members of religious orders or to address older people in the community. The same is true for aunt, uncle, and cousin. There may be a blood tie but, on the other hand, it could be a bond of affection.

Names identify individuals and as individuals changed so did their names. This is true not only for people but for the land as well. A modern example which illustrates both is David Grün who was born in Plonsk, Russia (now Poland), in 1886. He went to Palestine in 1906 where he lived under the name of David Green. When he died in 1973 his name was David Ben-Gurion and the land he died in was called Israel.

Reading and Reference Suggestions

Smith, Elston C.: *Dictionary of American Family Names.* New York, Harper & Row, 1956.

—————————. *Treasury of Name Lore: Sketches and Observations on the Names We Bear.* New York, Harper & Row, 1967.

Do We Have a Date?

Dating an event is sometimes more difficult than you expect, because there are a number of dating systems in use. The New Year can begin in autumn, mid-winter, or early spring depending on which of the various calendars is being used. Religious records and 18-century dates pose special problems.

LaSalle, Illinois 1907

Chicago, Illinois 1930

Chicago, Illinois 1895

We have gotten so used to the calendar we live with that it comes as a shock when we find out that George Washington was not born on February 22, 1732, but on February 11, 1731. We can be shaken up even more when we look into the whole matter of calendars and calendar reform. For example, just take the 18th century, the Age of Reason. At that time the Julian calendar and the Gregorian calendar were being used concurrently with the calendars for the Quakers, Jews, and Orientals. When was New Year? Did it start January 1, March 1, March 25, or sometime during the harvest season?

The calendar used by most people in the United States to conduct business today is the Gregorian calendar, named after Pope Gregory XIII who decreed its use in Catholic countries in 1582. Queen Elizabeth thought it was a good idea but the change never got through Parliament until 1752, and, when it did, it produced 50 years of legal wrangles.

In the English colonies, September 2, 1752, was followed by September 14. This meant that everyone born before September 2, 1752, and after February 29, 1700, was 11 days older. If they were born before February 29, 1700, they were only 10 days older because 1700 was not a leap year in the Gregorian calendar.

The Dutch in New Netherland never used the Julian calendar, having adopted the Gregorian calendar before they came over to America, and they continued using the Gregorian calendar in their private correspondence even after the English took over.

The Quakers, who believed in plain talk, called the months and the days of the week by their numerical names instead of those derived from heathen deities (for example, first day, ninth month). Until 1752, first month might be March or it might be January.

When the year started in late March (as it did in England before 1752), this meant that March 8, 1730, and March 28, 1731, were only 20 days apart. For example, you might find that a child was born April 14, 1740, and a note that its mother died in February 1740. Some people, however, were using January 1 as New Year's Day before 1752. To cut down on the confusion, double dating was used for dates that fell between January 1 and March 25 (inclusive). You might, for example, find dates given as December 25, 1710, January 12, 1710/11, March 20, 1710/11, March 27, 1711. The dates on which the Gregorian calendar was adopted vary widely: France, Spain, Portugal, and the Netherlands, 1582; the Catholic states of Germany, 1584; Poland, 1586; Hungary, 1587; the Protestant states of Germany and Switzerland, 1700; England and Sweden, 1752; China, 1912; Russia, 1917; Greece, 1923; and Turkey, 1928. Colonies used the same calendar as their mother countries.

Don't be surprised if some people got confused in changing their dates. In Western records, the longest year was the "Year of Confusion." This was 46 B.C. when Julius Caesar created a 445-day year in order to make the transition to his new calendar. The shortest month was September 1752, when the transition was made to the Gregorian calendar. It was only 19 days long.

What starting point do we use in counting years? The Romans used the traditional year of the city's founding, which was 753 B.C. Kings often used the year of their reign; George III, for example, used "in the Seventh Year of our Reign, Anno Dom. 1767." The current civil calendar is based on the supposed date of the birth of Christ, anno Domini meaning "in the year of the Lord."

The French had a revolutionary calendar between September 22, 1792, and 1806, when Napoleon abolished it, in which the months, all with new names, had 10-day weeks. The year started in September. If you have French connections who lived at that time, it is important to get the dates straight.

Many people still use separate calendars. The old Chinese calendar is a lunar calendar with alternating 29- and 30-day months. It begins in early February with an extra month added from time to time to keep the calendar in step with the solar year. The calendar has a 12-year cycle, and people using it will often give dates in terms of the year in the cycle during which the event took place. One has to do detective work to find which specific year in the civil calendar is meant. For example, 1977 is the Year of the Serpent, as was 1965 and 1893. The Year of the Serpent is always followed by the Year of the Horse (1978, 1966, 1894), the Ram (1979, 1967, 1895), the Monkey (1980, 1968, 1896), the Rooster (1981, 1969, 1897), the Dog (1982, 1970, 1898), the Boar (1983, 1971, 1899), the Rat (1984, 1972, 1900), the Ox (1985, 1973, 1901), the Tiger (1986, 1974, 1902), the Hare (1987, 1975, 1903), and the Dragon (1988, 1976, 1904).

The Jewish calendar is also a lunar calendar with 29- and 30-day months. It begins in the harvest season and is kept in step with the solar calendar by adding a "leap" month seven times in a 19-year cycle. The leap month, called Adar II, is tacked onto Adar in the 3rd, 6th, 8th, 11th, 14th, 17th, and 19th year of the cycle. The Jewish day starts at dusk which can vary geographically and by custom. In the summer, 7 PM can be the same day as 2 PM while in the winter it might be the next day. If working with Jewish records, it might be an idea to get a perennial sunrise-sundown calendar for a specific location from the U.S. Naval Observatory (Washington, DC 20390), since a daytime hour is the time between sunrise and sunset divided by 12. On longer days, an hour can be 75 minutes long. Jewish calendars run from September to September; some include the dates from the civil calendar. To get from the civil calendar to the Jewish calendar, subtract 1240 from the civil date and put a 5 in front of the remainder, but remember that you are about four months into the year. To get from the Jewish calendar to the civil calendar, strike out the 5 and add 1240 to the remainder; don't forget to make an adjustment for the time the New Year starts.

Where Do We Go From Here?

Now that you have made a good start, you will want to extend your efforts and continue the search. There are libraries and specialized groups devoted to family history. These sources and the suggested reading list can help you trace your roots further.

LaSalle, Illinois 1917

Chicago, Illinois 1898

After collecting and checking the information you have been able to get yourself and from the rest of the family — and getting it recorded on your charts — you may feel as if you have come up against a stone wall. Look over the material you have already collected and see if there is a clue you missed before. From time to time new records become available, and every so often it pays to go back and look again. Get a different perspective; try and look at your family from a different point of view. Read a book about the period or problem you are trying to solve. Ask yourself, "What would I have done back then?"

Re-check to make sure the date is right. An individual born in November 1900 will not appear in the 1900 census. Double-check that the place is right. For example, Wayne County, Ohio, in 1797 is not the same neck of the woods as Wayne County, Ohio, in 1977. In fact, the area that was Wayne County, Ohio, in 1797 is now Wayne County, Michigan. Have you been looking at the wrong record?

From time to time look at the photocopies you have made to see if they have begun to fade. Some are not permanent and should be recopied before they go blank.

You may want to try new approaches. You may want to *do* something. Plan a trip with maps and guidebooks to retrace the family travels. You might even take it! Visit or get a large-scale map of the spot where a member of your family lived. Take a ride and then walk around the area. If you have a large-scale map take a compass and draw a five-mile circle around the area and see if you find some more clues.

Chicago, Illinois 1920

Flushing, New York 1895

LaSalle, Illinois 1910

Elmhurst, Illinois 1947

Check the churches, schools, cemeteries, and courthouse. If you don't find anything, make a larger circle and start over.

Take pictures of all the spots you find that are associated with your family: the old farm, the apartment house, the school, and the cemetery. Get them for the record before "progress" catches up with them.

Sometimes it pays to advertise when you want to catch an elusive ancestor. You might put an ad in a local paper, a "family" magazine (a magazine devoted to a single family), or in the *Genealogical Helper*. You will get better results if you ask for a specific piece of information (such as the date of a marriage or death) rather than "all about" so-and-so. Be sure to give enough of the information you have collected so that so-and-so can be identified. You may find people who want to trade information. For family history buffs, pinning down a hard-to-find ancestor is more exciting than coming across a rare stamp or baseball card.

There are about as many ways to trace a family as there are to make a stew. Verify your records, have fun, keep smiling, and get out and dig!

Suggested Sources For Further Reading

The following list has been selected to show the scope of printed material available to help you trace your own roots. The card catalogue of your library will offer specialized resources for local history. The bibliographies and chapter references of genealogical handbooks will give you additional sources.

Directories

Ash, Lee (ed.): *Subject Collections: A Guide to Special Book Collections and Subject Emphases as Reported by University, College, Public and Special Libraries and Museums in the United States and Canada,* ed. 4 (lists location of library and name of person in charge). New York, R. R. Bowker, 1974.

Directory of Special Libraries and Information Centers, ed. 3. Detroit, Gale Research Co., 1976.

Fiske, Margaret (ed.): *Encyclopedia of Associations: Volume 1. National Organizations of the United States.* Detroit, Gale Research Co., 1976.

Hereditary Register of the United States of America. Washington DC, United States Hereditary Register, Inc., 1972.

Historical Societies and Agencies in the United States and Canada, ed. 10. Nashville, American Association for State and Local History, 1975.

Bibliographies

American and English Genealogies in the Library of Congress, ed. 2. Reprinted, Baltimore, Genealogical Publishing Co., 1967.

Filby, P. William: *American and British Genealogy and Heraldry: A Selected List of Books,* ed. 2. Chicago, American Library Association, 1975.

Kaminkow, Marion: *Genealogies in the Library of Congress: A Bibliography.* Baltimore, Magna Carta, 1972.

Munsell, Joel, Sons of: *Index to American Genealogies and to Genealogical Material Contained in All Works . . .* Reprinted, Baltimore, Genealogical Publishing Co., 1967.

Schreiner-Yantis, Netti (ed.): *Genealogical Books in Print.* Springfield, Pennsylvania, privately published, 1975.

Swem, E.G.: *Virginia Historical Index.* Gloucester, Massachusetts, Peter Smith, 1965.

Genealogical Booksellers and Publishers

Century Enterprises, P.O. Box 607, Huntsville, Arkansas 72740.

Deseret Book Co., 44 East South Temple, Salt Lake City, Utah 84102.

Everton Publishers, P.O. Box 368, Logan, Utah 84321.

Genealogical Publishing Co., 521-523 St. Paul Place, Baltimore, Maryland 21202.

Goodspeeds Book Shop, Inc., 18 Beacon St., Boston, Massachusetts 02108.

Forms and Other Supplies

Everton Publishers, P.O. Box 368, Logan, Utah 84321.

Deseret Book Co., 44 East South Temple, Salt Lake City, Utah 84102.

Genealogy Unlimited, Inc., 789 South Buffalo Grove Road, Buffalo Grove, Illinois 60090.

Ye Olde Genealogie Shoppe, 9430 Vandergriff Road, Indianapolis, Indiana 46239.

Genealogical Periodicals

American Genealogist, 1232 39th Street, Des Moines, Iowa 50311.

Genealogical Helper, Everton Publishers, P.O. Box 368, Logan, Utah 84321.

National Genealogical Society Quarterly, National Genealogical Society, 1921 Sunderland Place, N.W., Washington DC 20036.

Konrad, J.: *A Directory of Genealogical Periodicals,* ed. 2, 1977 (lists 290 periodicals published by societies, 94 periodicals published by individuals and firms, and 277 "one-name" family periodicals; P.O. Box 222, Munroe Falls, Ohio 44262).

Designing Your Own Coat of Arms

Heraldry is not only fascinating, it's great fun. It is a romantic art that goes back to the days of the great Gothic cathedrals and knightly tournaments. You can create your own coat of arms and use it as a personal identification — on bookplates, on pillows and hangings, or even on your own banner.

Crest

Wreath

Helmet

Mantling

Shield

Motto

DEO ET PATRIA OMNIA DEBEO

Basic elements of the coat of arms

In the course of tracing your roots, you may discover that your family possesses an authentic coat of arms. Even if you don't, however, you can enjoy designing your own. You will soon be fascinated by the lore of heraldry — the devising, recording, and study of coats of arms and their development.

Coats of arms developed in 12th-century Europe in order to identify armored knights at tournaments and on the field of battle. In time, this personal identification became a mark of ownership, labeling the knight's horse, his silver, and even his wife. A woman, except for a reigning sovereign, traditionally used the arms of her father or her husband displayed on a lozenge or diamond shape. Today, of course, a woman may design and use her own arms, but the coat is still displayed on a lozenge.

As the use of arms increased and became hereditary, disputes arose as to who could legitimately use a certain design. This required specialists to keep track of the designs in use, referee arguments, and authorize new coats. Richard III established the College of Arms in 1483 and the heralds have taken on these tasks ever since. If you have time and money and have led a relatively blameless life, you can apply to the College of Arms (Queen Victoria Street, London E.C.4) for an officially recognized coat of arms. They still feel responsible for the colonies.

It is unethical, and in some parts of the world illegal, to appropriate an existing coat of arms. Having the same last name as the rightful owner does not entitle you to use his arms. This right is governed by the laws of inheritance and descends only in the family tree. The crafty individuals who advertise, "Send us your last name and $10 and we will send you your family coat of arms ready for framing," are not following the rules. Unless you have information substantiating your right to the arms, you shouldn't use them. A coat of arms is as personal as a toothbrush, and only those close enough to the rightful owner to use his toothbrush should use his arms. (Irish coats are exceptions to this rule. According to the Irish heralds, everyone with the same last name can use the family coat.)

The language of heraldry is a mixture of Norman French, Latin, and English. Once you master the basic terms, you will find it is an efficient way of describing the visual picture of the arms in words. This verbal description is called the *blazon*.

A complete coat of arms, sometimes called an *achievement,* is usually made up of a *crest, wreath, mantle, helmet,* and *shield,* finished off with a *motto* or two. Peers, governmental units, and very large corporations often add *supporters* to hold the arms up and a piece of *ground* underneath for the supporters to stand on.

The Motto

The motto is a ribbon or tag on which is inscribed a hope, a war cry, or a statement of fact. It may be the family motto, the motto of an order or organization of which the owner is a member, or a saying characteristic of his interests. A motto is not essential. Some coats have none, while others have two, one beneath the shield and the other over the crest.

The Crest

The crest is the figure or symbol attached to the top of the helmet as an aid to identification. The subject is often, but not always, taken from the shield. Originally the crest was made of light wood or leather, and crests should be items that might realistically be attached to a helmet.

The Helmet

The helmet, or *helm,* was used to protect the knight's head in combat and, incidentally, to support his crest. In the 17th century rules (often ignored today) were set up to designate different helmets for different ranks of people. Sovereigns had barred gold helmets facing forward; peers had barred silver helmets facing sideways; knights had steel helmets facing forward with the visors open; and gentlemen had steel helmets facing sideways with the visors closed.

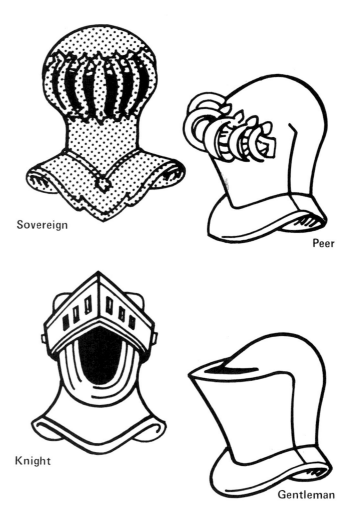

Sovereign

Peer

Knight

Gentleman

Helmets used to indicate rank

Six of the most important charges

Shields labeled: Chief, Chevron, Pale, Fess, Cross, Saltire

The Mantle

The mantle, or *lambrequin,* was originally a piece of material attached to the knight's helmet to protect him from the heat of the sun. Today its importance is in filling out the design. A mantle can be whole or much divided. The divided variety, sometimes called seaweed, is thought to represent struggle and hand-to-hand fighting.

The Wreath

The wreath, or *torse,* was a piece of twisted silk at the base of the crest that was used to attach the mantle to the helmet. The wreath is conventionally shown with six twists alternating the colors of the shield. It can be given a little shape, so that it doesn't look like a two-tone bread stick.

The Shield

The shield is the most important element in the coat of arms. While an individual can have a shield without a crest, the crest cannot exist without a shield. It is made up of the *field* (the surface or background) and the *charges* (the patterns or symbols drawn on the field). The shape of the field is limited only by the designer's taste.

The Field

Arms are described in terms of the wearer. For this reason, the *dexter* side (Latin for "right") appears to be on the left side of the viewer. The *sinister* side (Latin for "left") appears to be on the right. When you read a description, imagine that you are wearing the arms. The top portion of the shield is called the *chief* and the bottom the *base.* When the shield is divided into segments by lines it is said to be *party* or parted.

The Charges

When bands rather than lines are used to divide the field, the geometric shapes formed are charges called *ordinaries.* Some secondary patterns are subordinaries.

Canton

Lozenge

Escutcheon

Three subordinaries that are frequently seen

Heraldic Rose

Fleur-de-lis or Lily

Lion

Lion

Lion

Lion

Flowers and animals are often used as charges

A vast variety of designs can be placed on the field and the ordinaries. The most common of these charges are animals and flowers, but almost anything, animate or inanimate, will do. The lion is the most popular animal and is shown in a number of stances; roses and lilies are the most frequently used flowers.

Differences

Since a coat of arms belongs to an individual and not to a whole family, relatives of the rightful owner must modify their coats in certain ways (called *differencing*). The birth order of sons in England is conventionally indicated by marks of difference called *cadency* marks. When the oldest son inherits, he removes the mark of difference and uses the plain coat of arms.

The use of specific arms is restricted to blood heirs; an acknowledged bastard could use his father's coat provided that it carries a difference for illegitimacy. Some of these marks are the *wavy bordure* (border), the *compony bordure*, the *baton sinister*, and the

1. Label

2. Crescent

3. Molet

4. Martlet

5. Annulet

6. Fleur-de-lis

7. Rose

8. Cross Moline

9. Double Quatrefoil

Marks of difference for the first nine sons

Wavy Bordure

Compony Bordure

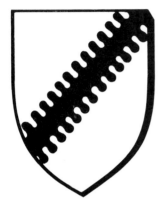

Bend Sinister

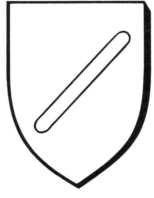

Baton Sinister

Bendlet Sinister

Marks indicating illegitimacy

Two links of chain are now used to show adoption

bendlet sinister. The bar sinister, a phrase sometimes associated with illegitimacy, does not exist, since a bar is always horizontal and, therefore, cannot be sinister or dexter. There are people who would rather be illegitimate somebodies than legitimate nobodies, and any individual who can prove descent from a royal bastard may be eligible for membership in the Descendants of the Illegitimate Sons and Daughters of the Kings of Britain. In recent years two links of chain have been used to indicate adoption.

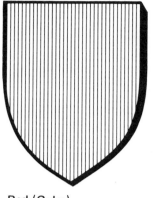

Red (Gules)

Blue (Azure)

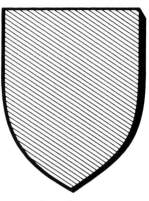

Green (Vert)

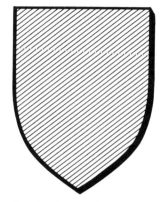

Purple (Purpure)

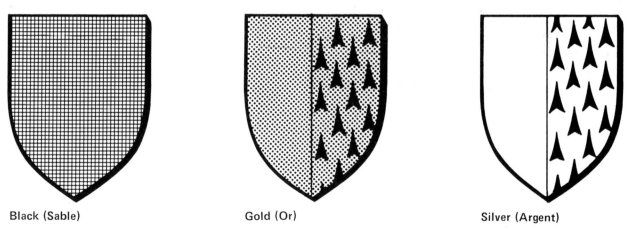

Black (Sable)

Gold (Or)

Silver (Argent)

Tinctures and the conventions used to indicate color in black-and-white pictures

The Tinctures

The colors used to enhance the design are called *tinctures*. The tinctures are made up of two metals — gold *(or)* and silver *(argent)*, usually shown as yellow and white; five colors — red *(gules)*, blue *(azure)*, green *(vert)*, purple *(purpure)*, and black *(sable)*; and two groups of furs — the *vair pattern* of alternate pieces of white and blue variously arranged and the *ermine patterns*, which can be black spots on white

Vair pattern   Vair pattern   Ermine

Ermines   Erminois   Pean

Furs may be displayed in vair or ermine patterns

(ermine), white spots on black *(ermines),* black spots on gold *(erminois),* or gold spots on black *(pean).* When the tinctures are shown in black-and-white drawings, certain conventions are used to show the colors. You can also draw lines to the various areas of the shield and write out the names or abbreviations of the colors (this is called *tricking*).

There is a great leeway in the choice of shade. The most important consideration is contrast. For this reason, a metal is usually displayed on a color, and a color is usually displayed on a metal. Furs may be used on either a color or a metal.

Designing Your Own Arms

In designing your own coat of arms, you will want to combine all these elements so that the coat represents you and no one else. To get ideas for your arms jot down your name, hobbies, occupation, zodiac sign, etc. Armstrong, Forrest, and Carpenter, for example, are easy to show graphically. A Little Leaguer might use, "Vert, a voided lozenge argent" — a green shield with white base paths on it (a voided lozenge is a hollow diamond shape); the crest might show an arm holding a bat, and the motto might be "Play ball!" Another sports enthusiast might choose,

"Vert, three tennis balls argent" with a motto reading "Next year, Wimbledon."

Give your imagination free rein and create several possible coats before deciding which one best expresses your personality. You can use your coat as a needlepoint or embroidery design and as a personal identification label (on bookplates, for example). You can even make your very own banner. Take two pieces of material 24 inches long by 24 inches wide and apply your design on each piece with acrylic paint or crayons. Before sewing the two pieces together, cover the design with a piece of brown paper and set the colors with a warm iron. An interlining will help your banner stand out when there is no breeze. Finish it off with fringe or thin braid.

Suggested Reading

Allcock, Hubert: *Heraldic Design: Its Origins, Ancient Forms, and Modern Use.* New York, Tudor Publishing Co., 1962.

Child, Heather: *Heraldic Design: A Handbook for Students.* London, G. Bell & Son, 1965.

Moncrieffe, Iain, and Pottinger, Don: *Simple Heraldry for Fun and Instruction.* London, Thomas Nelson & Sons, 1953.

ANCESTRY CHART

You	Your Parents	Your Grandparents	Your Great-Grandparents	Your Great-Great-Grandparents

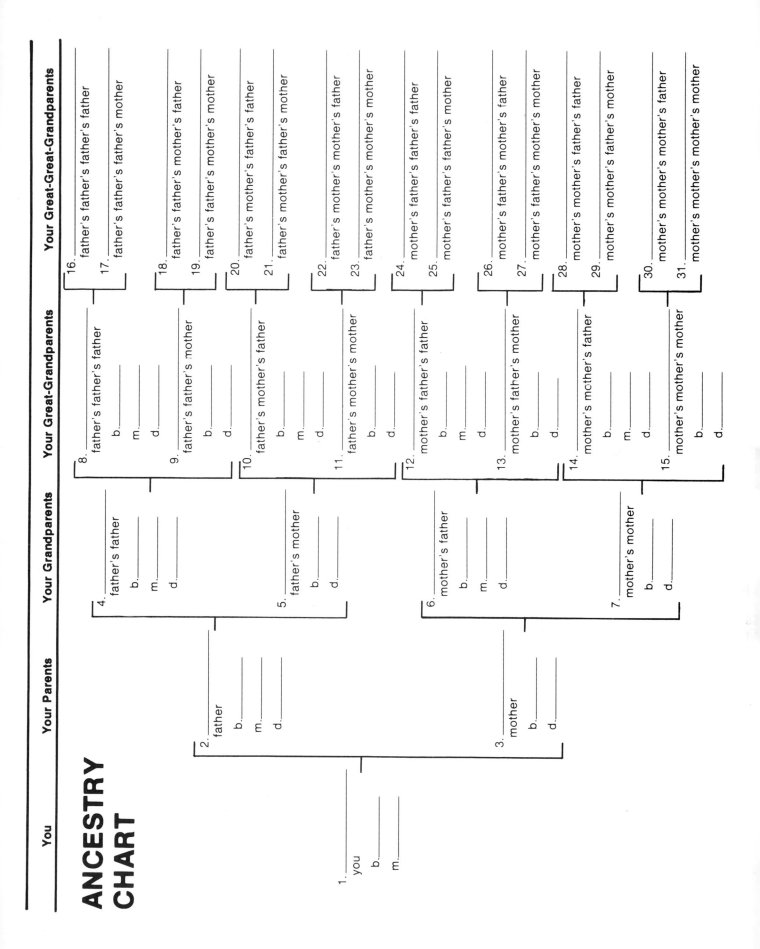

1. you
b.
m.

2. father
b.
m.
d.

3. mother
b.
d.

4. father's father
b.
m.
d.

5. father's mother
b.
d.

6. mother's father
b.
m.
d.

7. mother's mother
b.
d.

8. father's father's father
b.
m.
d.

9. father's father's mother
b.
d.

10. father's mother's father
b.
m.
d.

11. father's mother's mother
b.
d.

12. mother's father's father
b.
m.
d.

13. mother's father's mother
b.
d.

14. mother's mother's father
b.
m.
d.

15. mother's mother's mother
b.
d.

16. father's father's father's father
17. father's father's father's mother
18. father's father's mother's father
19. father's father's mother's mother
20. father's mother's father's father
21. father's mother's father's mother
22. father's mother's mother's father
23. father's mother's mother's mother
24. mother's father's father's father
25. mother's father's father's mother
26. mother's father's mother's father
27. mother's father's mother's mother
28. mother's mother's father's father
29. mother's mother's father's mother
30. mother's mother's mother's father
31. mother's mother's mother's mother

ANCESTRY CHART

You   **Your Parents**   **Your Grandparents**   **Your Great-Grandparents**   **Your Great-Great-Grandparents**

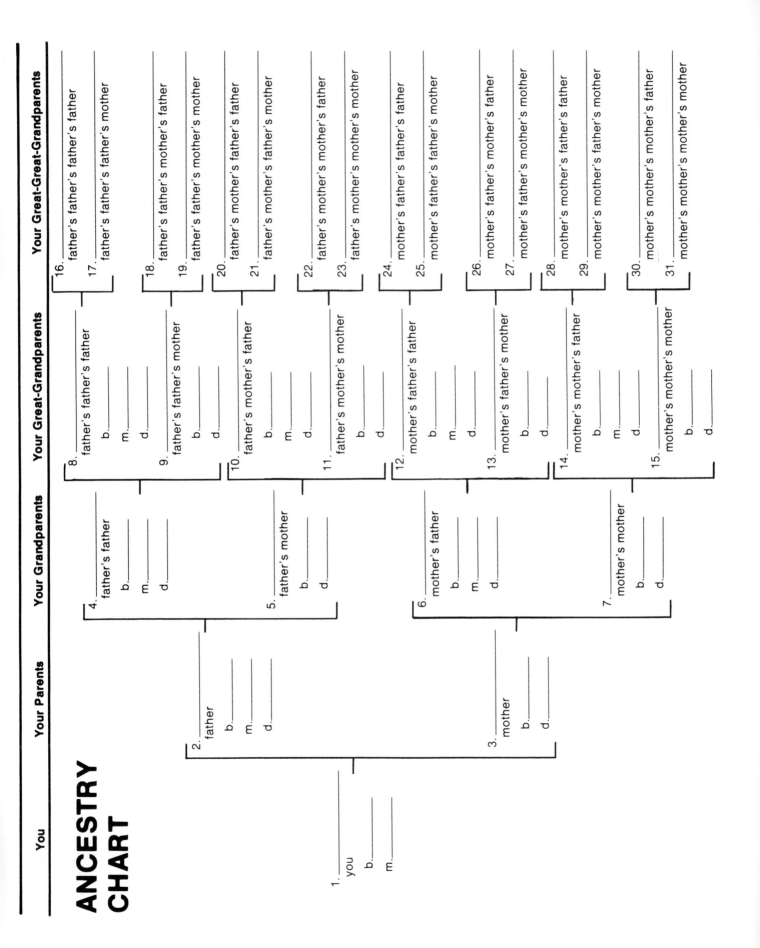

1. ___ you
b. ___
m. ___

2. ___ father
b. ___
m. ___
d. ___

3. ___ mother
b. ___
d. ___

4. ___ father's father
b. ___
m. ___
d. ___

5. ___ father's mother
b. ___
d. ___

6. ___ mother's father
b. ___
m. ___
d. ___

7. ___ mother's mother
b. ___
d. ___

8. ___ father's father's father
b. ___
m. ___
d. ___

9. ___ father's father's mother
b. ___
d. ___

10. ___ father's mother's father
b. ___
m. ___
d. ___

11. ___ father's mother's mother
b. ___
d. ___

12. ___ mother's father's father
b. ___
m. ___
d. ___

13. ___ mother's father's mother
b. ___
d. ___

14. ___ mother's mother's father
b. ___
m. ___
d. ___

15. ___ mother's mother's mother
b. ___
d. ___

16. ___ father's father's father's father
17. ___ father's father's father's mother
18. ___ father's father's mother's father
19. ___ father's father's mother's mother
20. ___ father's mother's father's father
21. ___ father's mother's father's mother
22. ___ father's mother's mother's father
23. ___ father's mother's mother's mother
24. ___ mother's father's father's father
25. ___ mother's father's father's mother
26. ___ mother's father's mother's father
27. ___ mother's father's mother's mother
28. ___ mother's mother's father's father
29. ___ mother's mother's father's mother
30. ___ mother's mother's mother's father
31. ___ mother's mother's mother's mother

60

INDIVIDUAL INFORMATION SHEET

No. on ancestry chart: _____

Name: _____

Nicknames and/or name changes: _____

Born: (Date) _____ (Place) _____

Father's name: _____ (see sheet No. _____)

Mother's maiden name: _____ (see sheet No. _____)

MARRIAGES

Married to:	Date	Place	Marriage ended by	Children
1. _____	_____	_____	_____	_____
2. _____	_____	_____	_____	_____
3. _____	_____	_____	_____	_____
4. _____	_____	_____	_____	_____

Distinguishing characteristics and health info: _____

_____

Schools attended: (elementary) _____; (high) _____;

(trade) _____; (college) _____

Social Security No.: _____

Jobs and occupations: _____

_____

Military service: _____

Photo or portrait: _____

Personal belongings; family stories and traditions: _____

_____

Additional sources of info: _____

_____

DOCUMENTATION FOR INDIVIDUAL INFORMATION SHEET

Legal name change (except by marriage):

Biographies:

Birth records:

Marriage records:

    First marriage:

    Second marriage:

    Third marriage:

    Fourth marriage:

Divorce records:

Religious affiliation(s):

Schools attended:

    Elementary:

    High school:

    Trade or vocational:

    College or university:

Jobs and occupations:

Clubs, lodges and societies:

Military service:

Residences:

Immigration/naturalization records:

Death records:

INDIVIDUAL INFORMATION SHEET

No. on ancestry chart: _____

Name: _____

Nicknames and/or name changes: _____

Born: (Date) _____ (Place) _____

Father's name: _____ (see sheet No. _____)

Mother's maiden name: _____ (see sheet No. _____)

MARRIAGES

Married to:	Date	Place	Marriage ended by	Children
1. _____	_____	_____	_____	_____
2. _____	_____	_____	_____	_____
3. _____	_____	_____	_____	_____
4. _____	_____	_____	_____	_____

Distinguishing characteristics and health info: _____

_____

Schools attended: (elementary) _____; (high) _____;

(trade) _____; (college) _____

Social Security No.: _____

Jobs and occupations: _____

_____

Military service: _____

Photo or portrait: _____

Personal belongings; family stories and traditions: _____

_____

Additional sources of info: _____

_____

DOCUMENTATION FOR INDIVIDUAL INFORMATION SHEET

Legal name change (except by marriage):

Biographies:

Birth records:

Marriage records:

First marriage:

Second marriage:

Third marriage:

Fourth marriage:

Divorce records:

Religious affiliation(s):

Schools attended:

Elementary:

High school:

Trade or vocational:

College or university:

Jobs and occupations:

Clubs, lodges and societies:

Military service:

Residences:

Immigration/naturalization records:

Death records:

INDIVIDUAL INFORMATION SHEET

No. on ancestry chart: _____

Name: _____

Nicknames and/or name changes: _____

Born: (Date) _____ (Place) _____

Father's name: _____ (see sheet No. _____)

Mother's maiden name: _____ (see sheet No. _____)

MARRIAGES

Married to:	Date	Place	Marriage ended by	Children
1. _____	_____	_____	_____	_____
2. _____	_____	_____	_____	_____
3. _____	_____	_____	_____	_____
4. _____	_____	_____	_____	_____

Distinguishing characteristics and health info: _____

_____

Schools attended: (elementary) _____; (high) _____;

(trade) _____; (college) _____

Social Security No.: _____

Jobs and occupations: _____

_____

Military service: _____

Photo or portrait: _____

Personal belongings; family stories and traditions: _____

_____

Additional sources of info: _____

_____

DOCUMENTATION FOR INDIVIDUAL INFORMATION SHEET

Legal name change (except by marriage):

Biographies:

Birth records:

Marriage records:

First marriage:

Second marriage:

Third marriage:

Fourth marriage:

Divorce records:

Religious affiliation(s):

Schools attended:

Elementary:

High school:

Trade or vocational:

College or university:

Jobs and occupations:

Clubs, lodges and societies:

Military service:

Residences:

Immigration/naturalization records:

Death records:

INDIVIDUAL INFORMATION SHEET

No. on ancestry chart: _____

Name: _____

Nicknames and/or name changes: _____

Born: (Date) _____ (Place) _____

Father's name: _____ (see sheet No. _____)

Mother's maiden name: _____ (see sheet No. _____)

MARRIAGES

Married to:	Date	Place	Marriage ended by	Children
1. _____	_____	_____	_____	_____
2. _____	_____	_____	_____	_____
3. _____	_____	_____	_____	_____
4. _____	_____	_____	_____	_____

Distinguishing characteristics and health info: _____

_____

Schools attended: (elementary) _____; (high) _____;

(trade) _____; (college) _____

Social Security No.: _____

Jobs and occupations: _____

_____

Military service: _____

Photo or portrait: _____

Personal belongings; family stories and traditions: _____

_____

Additional sources of info: _____

_____

DOCUMENTATION FOR INDIVIDUAL INFORMATION SHEET

Legal name change (except by marriage):

Biographies:

Birth records:

Marriage records:

    First marriage:

    Second marriage:

    Third marriage:

    Fourth marriage:

Divorce records:

Religious affiliation(s):

Schools attended:

    Elementary:

    High school:

    Trade or vocational:

    College or university:

Jobs and occupations:

Clubs, lodges and societies:

Military service:

Residences:

Immigration/naturalization records:

Death records:

INDIVIDUAL INFORMATION SHEET

No. on ancestry chart: _____

Name: _____

Nicknames and/or name changes: _____

Born: (Date) _____ (Place) _____

Father's name: _____ (see sheet No. _____)

Mother's maiden name: _____ (see sheet No. _____)

MARRIAGES

Married to:	Date	Place	Marriage ended by	Children
1. _____	_____	_____	_____	_____
2. _____	_____	_____	_____	_____
3. _____	_____	_____	_____	_____
4. _____	_____	_____	_____	_____

Distinguishing characteristics and health info: _____
_____

Schools attended: (elementary) _____; (high) _____;

(trade) _____; (college) _____

Social Security No.: _____

Jobs and occupations: _____
_____

Military service: _____

Photo or portrait: _____

Personal belongings; family stories and traditions: _____
_____

Additional sources of info: _____
_____

DOCUMENTATION FOR INDIVIDUAL INFORMATION SHEET

Legal name change (except by marriage):

Biographies:

Birth records:

Marriage records:

First marriage:

Second marriage:

Third marriage:

Fourth marriage:

Divorce records:

Religious affiliation(s):

Schools attended:

Elementary:

High school:

Trade or vocational:

College or university:

Jobs and occupations:

Clubs, lodges and societies:

Military service:

Residences:

Immigration/naturalization records:

Death records:

INDIVIDUAL INFORMATION SHEET

No. on ancestry chart: _____

Name: _____

Nicknames and/or name changes: _____

Born: (Date) _____ (Place) _____

Father's name: _____ (see sheet No. _____)

Mother's maiden name: _____ (see sheet No. _____)

MARRIAGES

Married to:	Date	Place	Marriage ended by	Children
1. _____	_____	_____	_____	_____
2. _____	_____	_____	_____	_____
3. _____	_____	_____	_____	_____
4. _____	_____	_____	_____	_____

Distinguishing characteristics and health info: _____

_____

Schools attended: (elementary) _____; (high) _____;

(trade) _____; (college) _____

Social Security No.: _____

Jobs and occupations: _____

_____

Military service: _____

Photo or portrait: _____

Personal belongings; family stories and traditions: _____

_____

Additional sources of info: _____

_____

DOCUMENTATION FOR INDIVIDUAL INFORMATION SHEET

Legal name change (except by marriage):

Biographies:

Birth records:

Marriage records:

    First marriage:

    Second marriage:

    Third marriage:

    Fourth marriage:

Divorce records:

Religious affiliation(s):

Schools attended:

    Elementary:

    High school:

    Trade or vocational:

    College or university:

Jobs and occupations:

Clubs, lodges and societies:

Military service:

Residences:

Immigration/naturalization records:

Death records:

INDIVIDUAL INFORMATION SHEET

No. on ancestry chart: _____

Name: _____

Nicknames and/or name changes: _____

Born: (Date) _____ (Place) _____

Father's name: _____ (see sheet No. _____)

Mother's maiden name: _____ (see sheet No. _____)

MARRIAGES

Married to:	Date	Place	Marriage ended by	Children
1. _____	_____	_____	_____	_____
2. _____	_____	_____	_____	_____
3. _____	_____	_____	_____	_____
4. _____	_____	_____	_____	_____

Distinguishing characteristics and health info: _____
_____

Schools attended: (elementary) _____; (high) _____;

(trade) _____; (college) _____

Social Security No.: _____

Jobs and occupations: _____
_____

Military service: _____

Photo or portrait: _____

Personal belongings; family stories and traditions: _____
_____

Additional sources of info: _____
_____

DOCUMENTATION FOR INDIVIDUAL INFORMATION SHEET

Legal name change (except by marriage):

Biographies:

Birth records:

Marriage records:

First marriage:

Second marriage:

Third marriage:

Fourth marriage:

Divorce records:

Religious affiliation(s):

Schools attended:

Elementary:

High school:

Trade or vocational:

College or university:

Jobs and occupations:

Clubs, lodges and societies:

Military service:

Residences:

Immigration/naturalization records:

Death records:

INDIVIDUAL INFORMATION SHEET

No. on ancestry chart: _____

Name: _____

Nicknames and/or name changes: _____

Born: (Date) _____ (Place) _____

Father's name: _____ (see sheet No. _____)

Mother's maiden name: _____ (see sheet No. _____)

MARRIAGES

Married to:	Date	Place	Marriage ended by	Children
1. _____	_____	_____	_____	_____
2. _____	_____	_____	_____	_____
3. _____	_____	_____	_____	_____
4. _____	_____	_____	_____	_____

Distinguishing characteristics and health info: _____
_____

Schools attended: (elementary) _____; (high) _____;

(trade) _____; (college) _____

Social Security No.: _____

Jobs and occupations: _____
_____

Military service: _____

Photo or portrait: _____

Personal belongings; family stories and traditions: _____
_____

Additional sources of info: _____
_____

DOCUMENTATION FOR INDIVIDUAL INFORMATION SHEET

Legal name change (except by marriage):

Biographies:

Birth records:

Marriage records:

  First marriage:

  Second marriage:

  Third marriage:

  Fourth marriage:

Divorce records:

Religious affiliation(s):

Schools attended:

  Elementary:

  High school:

  Trade or vocational:

  College or university:

Jobs and occupations:

Clubs, lodges and societies:

Military service:

Residences:

Immigration/naturalization records:

Death records:

INDIVIDUAL INFORMATION SHEET

No. on ancestry chart: _____

Name: _____

Nicknames and/or name changes: _____

Born: (Date) _____ (Place) _____

Father's name: _____ (see sheet No. _____)

Mother's maiden name: _____ (see sheet No. _____)

MARRIAGES

Married to:	Date	Place	Marriage ended by	Children
1. _____	_____	_____	_____	_____
2. _____	_____	_____	_____	_____
3. _____	_____	_____	_____	_____
4. _____	_____	_____	_____	_____

Distinguishing characteristics and health info: _____

_____

Schools attended: (elementary) _____; (high) _____;

(trade) _____; (college) _____

Social Security No.: _____

Jobs and occupations: _____

_____

Military service: _____

Photo or portrait: _____

Personal belongings; family stories and traditions: _____

_____

Additional sources of info: _____

_____

DOCUMENTATION FOR INDIVIDUAL INFORMATION SHEET

Legal name change (except by marriage):

Biographies:

Birth records:

Marriage records:

    First marriage:

    Second marriage:

    Third marriage:

    Fourth marriage:

Divorce records:

Religious affiliation(s):

Schools attended:

    Elementary:

    High school:

    Trade or vocational:

    College or university:

Jobs and occupations:

Clubs, lodges and societies:

Military service:

Residences:

Immigration/naturalization records:

Death records:

INDIVIDUAL INFORMATION SHEET

No. on ancestry chart: _____

Name: _____

Nicknames and/or name changes: _____

Born: (Date) _____ (Place) _____

Father's name: _____ (see sheet No. _____)

Mother's maiden name: _____ (see sheet No. _____)

MARRIAGES

Married to:	Date	Place	Marriage ended by	Children
1. _____	_____	_____	_____	_____
2. _____	_____	_____	_____	_____
3. _____	_____	_____	_____	_____
4. _____	_____	_____	_____	_____

Distinguishing characteristics and health info: _____
_____

Schools attended: (elementary) _____; (high) _____;

(trade) _____; (college) _____

Social Security No.: _____

Jobs and occupations: _____
_____

Military service: _____

Photo or portrait: _____

Personal belongings; family stories and traditions: _____
_____

Additional sources of info: _____
_____

DOCUMENTATION FOR INDIVIDUAL INFORMATION SHEET

Legal name change (except by marriage):

Biographies:

Birth records:

Marriage records:

   First marriage:

   Second marriage:

   Third marriage:

   Fourth marriage:

Divorce records:

Religious affiliation(s):

Schools attended:

   Elementary:

   High school:

   Trade or vocational:

   College or university:

Jobs and occupations:

Clubs, lodges and societies:

Military service:

Residences:

Immigration/naturalization records:

Death records:

INDIVIDUAL INFORMATION SHEET

No. on ancestry chart: _____

Name: _____

Nicknames and/or name changes: _____

Born: (Date) _____ (Place) _____

Father's name: _____ (see sheet No. _____)

Mother's maiden name: _____ (see sheet No. _____)

MARRIAGES

Married to:	Date	Place	Marriage ended by	Children
1. _____	_____	_____	_____	_____
2. _____	_____	_____	_____	_____
3. _____	_____	_____	_____	_____
4. _____	_____	_____	_____	_____

Distinguishing characteristics and health info: _____

_____

Schools attended: (elementary) _____; (high) _____;

(trade) _____; (college) _____

Social Security No.: _____

Jobs and occupations: _____

_____

Military service: _____

Photo or portrait: _____

Personal belongings; family stories and traditions: _____

_____

Additional sources of info: _____

_____

DOCUMENTATION FOR INDIVIDUAL INFORMATION SHEET

Legal name change (except by marriage):

Biographies:

Birth records:

Marriage records:

First marriage:

Second marriage:

Third marriage:

Fourth marriage:

Divorce records:

Religious affiliation(s):

Schools attended:

Elementary:

High school:

Trade or vocational:

College or university:

Jobs and occupations:

Clubs, lodges and societies:

Military service:

Residences:

Immigration/naturalization records:

Death records:

INDIVIDUAL INFORMATION SHEET

No. on ancestry chart: _____

Name: _____

Nicknames and/or name changes: _____

Born: (Date) _____ (Place) _____

Father's name: _____ (see sheet No. _____)

Mother's maiden name: _____ (see sheet No. _____)

MARRIAGES

Married to:	Date	Place	Marriage ended by	Children
1. _____	_____	_____	_____	_____
2. _____	_____	_____	_____	_____
3. _____	_____	_____	_____	_____
4. _____	_____	_____	_____	_____

Distinguishing characteristics and health info: _____

_____

Schools attended: (elementary) _____; (high) _____;

(trade) _____; (college) _____

Social Security No.: _____

Jobs and occupations: _____

_____

Military service: _____

Photo or portrait: _____

Personal belongings; family stories and traditions: _____

_____

Additional sources of info: _____

_____

DOCUMENTATION FOR INDIVIDUAL INFORMATION SHEET

Legal name change (except by marriage):

Biographies:

Birth records:

Marriage records:

    First marriage:

    Second marriage:

    Third marriage:

    Fourth marriage:

Divorce records:

Religious affiliation(s):

Schools attended:

    Elementary:

    High school:

    Trade or vocational:

    College or university:

Jobs and occupations:

Clubs, lodges and societies:

Military service:

Residences:

Immigration/naturalization records:

Death records:

INDIVIDUAL INFORMATION SHEET

No. on ancestry chart: _____

Name: _____

Nicknames and/or name changes: _____

Born: (Date) _____ (Place) _____

Father's name: _____ (see sheet No. _____)

Mother's maiden name: _____ (see sheet No. _____)

MARRIAGES

Married to:	Date	Place	Marriage ended by	Children
1. _____	_____	_____	_____	_____
2. _____	_____	_____	_____	_____
3. _____	_____	_____	_____	_____
4. _____	_____	_____	_____	_____

Distinguishing characteristics and health info: _____

_____

Schools attended: (elementary) _____; (high) _____;

(trade) _____; (college) _____

Social Security No.: _____

Jobs and occupations: _____

_____

Military service: _____

Photo or portrait: _____

Personal belongings; family stories and traditions: _____

_____

Additional sources of info: _____

_____

DOCUMENTATION FOR INDIVIDUAL INFORMATION SHEET

Legal name change (except by marriage):

Biographies:

Birth records:

Marriage records:

    First marriage:

    Second marriage:

    Third marriage:

    Fourth marriage:

Divorce records:

Religious affiliation(s):

Schools attended:

    Elementary:

    High school:

    Trade or vocational:

    College or university:

Jobs and occupations:

Clubs, lodges and societies:

Military service:

Residences:

Immigration/naturalization records:

Death records:

INDIVIDUAL INFORMATION SHEET

No. on ancestry chart: _____

Name: _____

Nicknames and/or name changes: _____

Born: (Date) _____ (Place) _____

Father's name: _____ (see sheet No. _____)

Mother's maiden name: _____ (see sheet No. _____)

MARRIAGES

Married to:	Date	Place	Marriage ended by	Children
1. _____	_____	_____	_____	_____
2. _____	_____	_____	_____	_____
3. _____	_____	_____	_____	_____
4. _____	_____	_____	_____	_____

Distinguishing characteristics and health info: _____

_____

Schools attended: (elementary) _____; (high) _____;

(trade) _____; (college) _____

Social Security No.: _____

Jobs and occupations: _____

_____

Military service: _____

Photo or portrait: _____

Personal belongings; family stories and traditions: _____

_____

Additional sources of info: _____

_____

DOCUMENTATION FOR INDIVIDUAL INFORMATION SHEET

Legal name change (except by marriage):

Biographies:

Birth records:

Marriage records:

    First marriage:

    Second marriage:

    Third marriage:

    Fourth marriage:

Divorce records:

Religious affiliation(s):

Schools attended:

    Elementary:

    High school:

    Trade or vocational:

    College or university:

Jobs and occupations:

Clubs, lodges and societies:

Military service:

Residences:

Immigration/naturalization records:

Death records:

FAMILY INFORMATION SHEET

Family name: _____

Husband's name: _____ No. on ancestry chart: _____

    Date of birth: _____ Birthplace: _____

    Date of death: _____ Place of death: _____

    Date of burial: _____ Place of burial: _____

    Married _____ times; this marriage was No. _____.

    Father's name: _____ Mother's maiden name: _____

Wife's maiden name: _____ No. on ancestry chart: _____

Date of birth: _____ Birthplace: _____

Date of death: _____ Place of death: _____

Date of burial: _____ Place of burial: _____

Married _____ times; this marriage was No. _____.

Father's name: _____ Mother's maiden name: _____

Date of this marriage: _____; Place of this marriage: _____

Children of this marriage in order of birth (note multiple births):

Name	Born		Died		Married		
	Date	Where	Date	Where	Date	Where	To Whom
A.							
B.							
C.							
D.							
E.							
F.							
G.							
H.							

DOCUMENTATION FOR FAMILY INFORMATION SHEET

Children of: _____

See individual information sheet No. _____ for Child _____

Child A	Child E
Birth:	Birth:
Death:	Death:
Burial:	Burial:
Marriages:	Marriages:

Child B	Child F
Birth:	Birth:
Death:	Death:
Burial:	Burial:
Marriages:	Marriages:

Child C	Child G
Birth:	Birth:
Death:	Death:
Burial:	Burial:
Marriages:	Marriages:

Child D	Child H
Birth:	Birth:
Death:	Death:
Burial:	Burial:
Marriages:	Marriages:

Additional sources and notes:

FAMILY INFORMATION SHEET

Family name: _____

Husband's name: _____ No. on ancestry chart: _____

    Date of birth: _____ Birthplace: _____

    Date of death: _____ Place of death: _____

    Date of burial: _____ Place of burial: _____

    Married _____ times; this marriage was No. _____.

    Father's name: _____ Mother's maiden name: _____

Wife's maiden name: _____ No. on ancestry chart: _____

    Date of birth: _____ Birthplace: _____

    Date of death: _____ Place of death: _____

    Date of burial: _____ Place of burial: _____

    Married _____ times; this marriage was No. _____.

    Father's name: _____ Mother's maiden name: _____

Date of this marriage: _____; Place of this marriage: _____

Children of this marriage in order of birth (note multiple births):

Name	Born		Died		Married		
	Date	Where	Date	Where	Date	Where	To Whom
A.							
B.							
C.							
D.							
E.							
F.							
G.							
H.							

DOCUMENTATION FOR FAMILY INFORMATION SHEET

Children of: _____

See individual information sheet No. _____ for Child _____

Child A

Birth:

Death:

Burial:

Marriages:

Child E

Birth:

Death:

Burial:

Marriages:

Child B

Birth:

Death:

Burial:

Marriages:

Child F

Birth:

Death:

Burial:

Marriages:

Child C

Birth:

Death:

Burial:

Marriages:

Child G

Birth:

Death:

Burial:

Marriages:

Child D

Birth:

Death:

Burial:

Marriages:

Child H

Birth:

Death:

Burial:

Marriages:

Additional sources and notes:

FAMILY INFORMATION SHEET

Family name: _____

Husband's name: _____ No. on ancestry chart: _____

    Date of birth: _____ Birthplace: _____

    Date of death: _____ Place of death: _____

    Date of burial: _____ Place of burial: _____

    Married _____ times; this marriage was No. _____.

    Father's name: _____ Mother's maiden name: _____

Wife's maiden name: _____ No. on ancestry chart: _____

    Date of birth: _____ Birthplace: _____

    Date of death: _____ Place of death: _____

    Date of burial: _____ Place of burial: _____

    Married _____ times; this marriage was No. _____.

    Father's name: _____ Mother's maiden name: _____

Date of this marriage: _____; Place of this marriage: _____

Children of this marriage in order of birth (note multiple births):

| Name | Born | | Died | | Married | | |
	Date	Where	Date	Where	Date	Where	To Whom
A.							
B.							
C.							
D.							
E.							
F.							
G.							
H.							

DOCUMENTATION FOR FAMILY INFORMATION SHEET

Children of: _____

See individual information sheet No. _____ for Child _____

Child A

Birth:

Death:

Burial:

Marriages:

Child E

Birth:

Death:

Burial:

Marriages:

Child B

Birth:

Death:

Burial:

Marriages:

Child F

Birth:

Death:

Burial:

Marriages:

Child C

Birth:

Death:

Burial:

Marriages:

Child G

Birth:

Death:

Burial:

Marriages:

Child D

Birth:

Death:

Burial:

Marriages:

Child H

Birth:

Death:

Burial:

Marriages:

Additional sources and notes:

FAMILY INFORMATION SHEET

Family name: _____

Husband's name: _____ No. on ancestry chart: _____

    Date of birth: _____ Birthplace: _____

    Date of death: _____ Place of death: _____

    Date of burial: _____ Place of burial: _____

    Married _____ times; this marriage was No. _____.

    Father's name: _____ Mother's maiden name: _____

Wife's maiden name: _____ No. on ancestry chart: _____

    Date of birth: _____ Birthplace: _____

    Date of death: _____ Place of death: _____

    Date of burial: _____ Place of burial: _____

    Married _____ times; this marriage was No. _____.

    Father's name: _____ Mother's maiden name: _____

Date of this marriage: _____; Place of this marriage: _____

Children of this marriage in order of birth (note multiple births):

Name	Born		Died		Married		
	Date	Where	Date	Where	Date	Where	To Whom
A.							
B.							
C.							
D.							
E.							
F.							
G.							
H.							

DOCUMENTATION FOR FAMILY INFORMATION SHEET

Children of: _____

See individual information sheet No. _____ for Child _____

Child A

Birth:

Death:

Burial:

Marriages:

Child E

Birth:

Death:

Burial:

Marriages:

Child B

Birth:

Death:

Burial:

Marriages:

Child F

Birth:

Death:

Burial:

Marriages:

Child C

Birth:

Death:

Burial:

Marriages:

Child G

Birth:

Death:

Burial:

Marriages:

Child D

Birth:

Death:

Burial:

Marriages:

Child H

Birth:

Death:

Burial:

Marriages:

Additional sources and notes:

FAMILY INFORMATION SHEET

Family name: _____

Husband's name: _____ No. on ancestry chart: _____

    Date of birth: _____ Birthplace: _____

    Date of death: _____ Place of death: _____

    Date of burial: _____ Place of burial: _____

    Married _____ times; this marriage was No. _____.

    Father's name: _____ Mother's maiden name: _____

Wife's maiden name: _____ No. on ancestry chart: _____

    Date of birth: _____ Birthplace: _____

    Date of death: _____ Place of death: _____

    Date of burial: _____ Place of burial: _____

    Married _____ times; this marriage was No. _____.

    Father's name: _____ Mother's maiden name: _____

Date of this marriage: _____; Place of this marriage: _____

Children of this marriage in order of birth (note multiple births):

Name	Born		Died		Married		
	Date	Where	Date	Where	Date	Where	To Whom
A.							
B.							
C.							
D.							
E.							
F.							
G.							
H.							

DOCUMENTATION FOR FAMILY INFORMATION SHEET

Children of: _____

See individual information sheet No. _____ for Child _____

	Child A		Child E
Birth:		Birth:	
Death:		Death:	
Burial:		Burial:	
Marriages:		Marriages:	

	Child B		Child F
Birth:		Birth:	
Death:		Death:	
Burial:		Burial:	
Marriages:		Marriages:	

	Child C		Child G
Birth:		Birth:	
Death:		Death:	
Burial:		Burial:	
Marriages:		Marriages:	

	Child D		Child H
Birth:		Birth:	
Death:		Death:	
Burial:		Burial:	
Marriages:		Marriages:	

Additional sources and notes: